OTHER BOOKS BY HENRY B. ROTHBLATT

As Co-Author with F. Lee Bailey:

Defending the Juvenile and Young Offender
Cross-Examination in Criminal Cases
Handling Misdemeanor Cases
The Complete Manual of Criminal Forms, Volumes I and II
Fundamentals of Criminal Advocacy
Crimes of Violence: Rape and Other Sex Crimes
Successful Techniques for Criminal Trials
Investigation and Preparation of Criminal Cases
Defending Business and White Collar Crimes

As Co-Author with Robert L. Fish:

A Handy Death (fiction)

As Co-Author with Robin Moore:

Court Martial (fiction)

As Author:

Criminal Law of New York: The Revised Penal Law
Criminal Law of New York: The Criminal Procedure Law
Handbook of Evidence for Criminal Trials

HENRY B. ROTHBLATT

"That Damned Lawyer"

FOREWORD B

DODD, ME

N

Library of Congress Cataloging in Publication Data:

Rothblatt, Henry B.
  "That damned lawyer."

  1. Rothblatt, Henry B.   2. Lawyers—United States—
Biography.   I. Title.
KF373.R677A35   1983   349.73′092′4 [B]   82-25155
ISBN 0-89696-198-2   347.300924 [B]

TO

Pat Henry and Donna

Contents

Acknowledgments

OVER many years I have received help, criticism, and guidance from many persons and sources. Many people I have completely forgotten.

This book would not be complete without expressing my tribute and debt to those who have helped me in my career and have assisted me directly and indirectly in the writing of this manuscript.

My daughter, Henrietta Santo, contributed in countless ways, particularly in her expertise in the fields of lie detection and human deception.

My partners and associates, Jon Rothblatt, Joseph Seijas, and Judge Louis Rosenthal, furnished advice and help.

F. Lee Bailey of Boston; the late Jake Ehrlich; John Burgess; Melvin Belli of San Francisco; Percy Forman; the late William F. Walsh; Clyde Woody of Houston, Texas; Stanley Preiser of Charleston, West Virginia; and Harald Price Fahringer of New York, outstanding trial lawyers, contributed friendship and counsel.

I am also indebted to Judge Herbert Altman, Judge Miriam Altman, Sharon Haddock Anson, Abraham Eckstein, Michael Brodsky, and Dolores Kirk for their tremendous assistance.

My special thanks also to Dean Donald Shapiro and the faculty and staff of New York Law School for their friendship and help.

My deep gratitude goes to Joe Vergara and Ralph Bass for their enormous help in creating and editing this manuscript.

Foreword

WHEN I was preparing to leave for Vietnam to defend Captain Robert F. Marasco of the Green Berets against a murder charge, I found Henry Rothblatt there ahead of me. He was busily defending a related Green Beret case. I soon discovered that his efforts on behalf of the Berets had uncovered so much useful evidence and built up so strong a case that a good share of my job was already done for me.

Knowing Rothblatt as I do, this didn't surprise me. I have worked side by side with him on many challenging cases and look forward to sharing many more with him in the future.

The Big Judge in the Sky favored Henry with boundless energy and curiosity, along with a passion for the underdog. When asked, he quickly sprang to the defense of the accused My Lai soldiers and the Watergate Cubans. He did as much for numerous unknowns charged with serious crimes. Whether a client is accused of murder or of disturbing the peace, Rothblatt can be relied on to pull out all the stops to get the best possible disposition of his case. He is always ready to give that extra hour to research, to question that final witness, file that unexpected motion—all in the interests of his clients. Their rights are sacred to him, as they should be.

Aspects of criminal law today are much on everyone's mind. We all want effective law enforcement. We insist on protecting our civil rights. Questions about plea bargaining and about insanity defenses stir deep emotions. People wonder about the fairness of bail, the dangers inherent in parole. We worry about social and economic inequities and their impact on crime. In this churning climate, it is vital to have dedicated lawyers like Henry Rothblatt.

In this book, you will have the opportunity to watch a master craftsman at work. You will follow him as he develops his strategies, plans his defenses, and fights his court battles. As the story unfolds, you will begin to understand why so many of us—his fellow lawyers—consider Henry Rothblatt a "lawyer's lawyer." I am proud to have his friendship.

F. LEE BAILEY

Introduction

THE title of this book comes from an unflattering incident in my practice which, for some perverse reason, continues to amuse me. It may sound too coincidental to be true, but it actually happened.

I had just managed to obtain a doctor's acquittal in an abortion death case. It had seemed certain that the doctor-defendant would lose his license along with his freedom.

Right after the jury brought in its verdict, and while the doctor's friends were still congratulating him, I heard him say, "That damned lawyer. He must think I'm Rockefeller."

The next day, a reporter friend who had covered the trial dropped in at my office. He relayed one or two more compliments. From the judge: "I should have held that damned lawyer in contempt." From a juror: "Did you ever see a more egotistical s.o.b. than that damned lawyer?"

To these gentlemen I am indebted for my title. I must add congratulations to the juror on his character analysis and assure him that the criminal lawyer who does not have a man-sized ego (I like to call it self-confidence) will quickly succumb to ulcers.

Working on this book, I have had cause to look back on my four eventful decades of defending unpopular causes, becoming immersed in controversial issues, and of late, playing a middle-aged David against the Establishment Goliath. This retrospective look convinces me that we are now living in the most challenging time ever for a criminal lawyer.

As exciting as the practice of criminal law is, you must expect a few minor drawbacks. For one, too often you don't

13

get paid while your relieved client, exhausted by the trial, no doubt, recuperates in the Bahamas.

Also, no matter how brilliantly you perform for a client, he is not likely to send other clients to you. If a real estate, negligence or other civil law practitioner does a good job, he is sure to be recommended. But no one ever says to a friend in trouble, "Go to Henry Rothblatt. He got me out of a rape, sodomy, and indecent exposure jam." Most likely, he hopes his friend doesn't know about the rape, sodomy, and indecent exposure and is working hard to forget it himself.

But other attorneys know who the leading criminal lawyers are and they do send clients, including these days, White House aides, bank presidents, top-ranking politicians, and dynamic business leaders suspected of being a bit too dynamic. Some of these attorneys say that they don't want to be involved in the grimy aspects of criminal law, which they visualize as being grimier than they actually are. Most acknowledge that they just don't know the ropes.

Criminal law is challenging because it's a living thing, constantly evolving. Lawyers must evolve and grow along with it. These days, there are a number of ideas and trends abroad that may drastically alter and reshape the way a criminal lawyer performs his duties, inside and outside of the courtroom.

There is a growing controversy over the use of "forensic psychiatry"—the use of psychiatrists as expert witnesses in our courtrooms to help decide questions of "temporary insanity."

Dr. Alan A. Stone, professor of law at Harvard Law School and professor of psychiatry at Harvard Medical School, points out that the "public has long believed that a defense of insanity, particularly temporary insanity, allows for a crime that is perfect in the sense that it goes unpunished."

Not so, counters Dr. Stone. Historically, those found guilty by reason of insanity in both England and America "have with rare exceptions been confined for the rest of their lives in the wretched institutions that serve the criminally insane."

In more recent times that deplorable situation has been corrected, so much so, as reported by Dr. Stone, that "Several jurisdictions have held that after a person is found not guilty by reason of insanity, a new hearing must be convened to determine whether the person is then civilly committable. Still, this is not so easily accomplished. Persons must be proved beyond a reasonable doubt to be both mentally ill and dangerous and they are eligible for a periodic review of their condition. Unfortunately, neither psychiatrists nor anyone else can prove that someone is still dangerous."

Meanwhile, I find myself miffed by an event in my own state, New York, that seems to me to be a potential disaster. The New York State Department of Mental Hygiene would like to see the plea of not guilty by reason of insanity entirely abolished. In its stead, the department is recommending adoption of a "diminished capacity" rule. Under this rule, evidence of abnormal mental condition could be used only to reduce the severity of the crime charged. In other words, a homicide charge that requires "an intentional act" for conviction could be reduced to manslaughter, which demands only "reckless" behavior to establish guilt.

Among other worrisome developments, the Supreme Court shows alarming tendencies to pay more attention to Establishment petitions than to the due process rights of defendants. There is also the growing clamor in some states for an end to plea bargaining, about which much will be said later, and uneasy questions remain about the role of undercover agents, and the vexing problems involved in entrapment.

To be successful in court, the criminal lawyer should really have eyes in back of his head. He has to keep up with every important court ruling in the nation, with the provisions of the new Federal Criminal Code, with efforts to reform the grand jury system, and a few other unfolding dramas.

There is more than enough to do, so I really didn't have time to get upset when Chief Justice Warren Burger declared that about half of the nation's lawyers are incompetent to try cases.

This did, however, upset the American Bar Association. William B. Spann, Jr. of the ABA called a press conference and said that he thought the figure should be closer to 20 percent. I thought that Mr. Spann was prejudiced in favor of his fellow lawyers.

Justice Burger also found time in 1977 to warn the nation that unless new ways were found to settle disputes without going to court, the country could be "overrun by hordes of lawyers hungry as locusts."

I have no interest in discussing the proportion of competent criminal lawyers. One thing I am sure of. Mere competence is not enough. The criminal lawyer is defending human freedom and human life against the State's enormous power. There is no higher challenge under the law, and no nobler responsibility.

HENRY B. ROTHBLATT

"THAT DAMNED LAWYER"

ONE

A Lawyer Is Born

My FATHER planted the notion in my head when I was a youngster in grade school. He was a cabinet worker by trade—whenever there was cabinet work to be had. He shared the manual worker's envy of the professional. And he had definite ideas about which profession he favored.

"Doctors don't have it so good," he told me one day. "They work with sick people, examine them for all kinds of unpleasant diseases, stick their fingers in mouths, rectums . . . Dentists too have a nasty job—standing up all day, staring into smelly mouths, torturing people, drilling little holes in rotten teeth. But lawyers, they have the life. Nice clothes, nice offices with books all around. And they get paid to talk nice to judges and juries and sound intelligent. Now that's my idea of a good job for you!"

He was forced to confess that I didn't exactly "talk nice," but he pointed out that I did have a strong voice, and God knows I loved to argue and would debate anybody on any subject. He was sure that all this showed keen aptitude for the law.

At the time we lived one block from the Bronx Magistrate's Court. Whether my father's brainwashing was responsible I'm not sure. In any case, summer vacations often found me sitting in the nearby courtroom watching the judges and juries at work. I marveled at the stream of accused humanity parading through. I was struck by the court's power to change a person's life, by the variety and intensity of passions that drove people to crime.

Some of the accused, I realized, were mentally sick and needed help. Some—the habitual criminals—were street-wise and court-wise and difficult if not impossible to help. Others seemed little different from me and my friends; they were decent enough kids, in trouble for the first time. Watching their scared young faces I wondered what would happen to them. Would they recognize their mistakes and overcome them? Or would they go on to bigger and better mistakes?

I was soon able to pick out the superior lawyers—those who worked hard to help their clients. And I learned to spot the obvious errors made by the poorer lawyers.

The lawyers I admired seemed to be in control of the case every step of the way. They were especially skillful in cross-examination. They never seemed to ask a question of a hostile witness unless they knew pretty well what answer they'd get. The inexperienced lawyer, on the other hand, rambled along asking pointless questions until he put his client behind the eight ball.

One day, I watched a defendant's lawyer let his client down badly. The defendant was charged with killing an alcoholic acquaintance.

"Did you ever hear the deceased say anything about my client?" the lawyer asked a hostile witness, possibly because he could think of nothing better to do.

"Yes, I did," was the response.

Then, for some unfathomable reason, the lawyer persisted. "What were his exact words?"

Even I sensed that there was no way this question could help his client. The witness drew himself up and intoned solemnly, " 'I know he wants to kill me, and he will, too. But when I'm dead, he'll pay for it.' "

The jurors could hardly believe their ears. It was the defendant's own lawyer who had brought out this damning testimony! The prosecutor himself couldn't have done any better. The deceased, speaking from the grave, proved to be an excellent prophet.

As I watched case after case, I became convinced that one day I would be a lawyer. I would emulate the best lawyers and I would avoid all the mistakes I was watching daily.

I constantly run into people who don't share my father's

admiration of lawyers, especially of criminal lawyers. "How can you represent those goons and murderers?" they ask.

"Easy," I tell them. "They're my clients."

Or I tell them of my legal friend who says that his whopping big fee is his way of punishing his wayward clients.

If I am feeling philosophic, I explain that our Anglo-American system of justice holds that *everyone* has certain rights guaranteed by the Constitution. Even an armed robber or murderer is protected. He is entitled to counsel. And our system maintains that it is wrong for the police to smash a man's face during interrogation, to force a confession or to keep anyone in jail for months before giving him an opportunity to present his version of events.

Our system, let's remember, was built on a deep mistrust of authority and power in society. The writers of our Constitution felt it was vital to set up safeguards to protect the accused against the machinery of the State. It was, in their view, better to create a system which allowed an occasional guilty person to go free than one in which an occasional innocent person was found guilty.

In this search for justice with fairness, the criminal lawyer has a pivotal role to play. It is his responsibility to see that the accused is not unfairly deprived of his freedom. By protecting defendants, whether guilty or innocent, from the abuse of power by the State, the criminal lawyer protects us all.

I feel strongly that our system of safeguards is correct and I deeply appreciate my duty as a criminal lawyer. Even so, I am bound to admit that there is another and stronger reason why I prefer criminal practice.

Frankly, I just can't see myself as a tax lawyer dedicated to saving Exxon a few paltry millions, or as a corporation counsel overseeing company legal policies, or as a government lawyer compiling tons of self-serving reports for federal agencies. There's nothing wrong with any of this; but to me it all seems so bloodless.

In criminal law you rub shoulders with raw humanity with all the emotions showing. You deal with people faced with the loss of liberty or even with death. You meet people with every kind of psychological problem. Too much drinking, addiction, poverty, perversion. Kids just beginning to grow up. Spoiled rich kids, despairing minority kids. The whole gamut.

You learn about the pressures of life and how to deal with human beings under stress. Sometimes you help people against the injustices of society. Imagine the satisfaction of getting a youngster released who has been unjustly charged, or is a victim of mistaken identity—perhaps set up by a policeman needing a "collar" to fill his quota.

I remember a young black boy I defended. I'll call him Jim. He had a terrible record and so did all his brothers and sisters, along with his father. I had defended all of them at one time or another.

Jim was arrested for robbery along with one of his brothers and three other boys. The victim, a garage owner, identified all five of the boys. It seemed an open and shut case.

Jim's mother came to see me, obviously upset. "Mr. Rothblatt, you've got to help Jim," she said, tears in her eyes, "I know he's innocent."

I'd heard this too often before from too many protective mothers. "How can you be sure?" I asked.

"Because he was home with me that night. Jim's brother *was* involved. He's guilty, but not Jim."

Her words had the ring of truth. Besides, what other reason could she have for defending Jim and not his brother? I decided to do what I could for Jim, and his mother.

Jim's brother and the others took a guilty plea but I refused to let Jim plead guilty. I told the disapproving judge, "Under no circumstances will my client plead guilty. The boy is innocent. It's a case of mistaken identity. I insist on a trial to prove my client's innocence."

I questioned Jim's brother and the other three boys and finally managed to learn the name of their companion in the robbery. It was not Jim. His mother had told the truth. I got a subpoena for the real accomplice to appear in court on the day of the trial.

During my cross-examination of the victim, I pointed out the boy I'd subpoenaed. "Did you ever see that boy before?" I asked him.

"No, no!" he said.

But by now the D.A. was having second thoughts. When court recessed, he did some checking on his own and ended up taking the accomplice into custody. The boy soon confessed.

Upbeat note. Jim never got into trouble again. Except in law, how could I ever enjoy the satisfaction I felt in helping to save that innocent youngster?

Having said this, I'm forced to admit that trial law holds another powerful attraction for me. It offers a continuous stage. Like most courtroom lawyers, I'm a bit of a performer at heart. I'm at home at the center of the human dramas being played out in court. I enjoy pitting my skills against others, using my ability to think on my feet, to analyze, to weigh and finally to persuade. The legal contest provides endless intellectual challenge and emotional satisfaction. Call it an ego trip, love of showmanship, exhibitionism. Whatever it is, I thrive on it. And I'll bet that my father suspected I would right from the start.

TWO

The Green Berets Under Fire

On A SHELF in my office sits a bust of Voltaire sporting a green beret tilted at a rakish angle. Whenever I feel tired or discouraged, or when powerful forces seem to be ganging up on a client, I look over at old Voltaire with his strange head-gear and I'm refreshed.

Members of the U.S. Army Fifth Special Forces Group— The Green Berets—presented the beret to me after I defended them against a murder charge by the Army.

I became involved in the case by accident. Captain John S. Berry, one of the Army officers representing the Green Beret defendants, had read several of my books on criminal law. He and his associates, Captain John W. Hart, Captain Myron D. Stutzman and Major Martin Linsky, had begun to worry about fulfilling their responsibilities. They never suggested as much, but I'm convinced that they were uneasy about how far they could buck the system in defending their clients. The system, in this instance, was General Creighton Abrams, Jr., commanding general of the U.S. Army in Vietnam.

When the Green Beret lawyers and defendants agreed that they needed a civilian lawyer, Captain Berry wrote me a letter asking me to represent Major David Crew, Captain Leland Brumley and Chief Warrant Officer Edward Boyle. It was understood also that I would assist in defending the other accused: Colonel Robert B. Rheault, Major Thomas E. Middleton, Jr., Captain Robert F. Marasco, Captain Budge E. Williams and Sergeant First Class Alvin L. Smith, Jr.

All of these men were members of the Green Berets. They were charged with the murder on June 20, 1969 of Thai Khac

Chuyen, a Vietnamese national, and of conspiracy to commit murder.

Before arriving in Vietnam I had serious doubts about the lawyer-officers of the Judge Advocate General's office. Never dewy-eyed about humanity, I wondered whether I'd be working with genuine colleagues or with stooges for the brass. After a few days with Captain Berry and his fellow lawyers, I was deeply ashamed of my suspicions. These men put their careers on the line to live up to their oaths as lawyers.

If General Abrams didn't like me, I could tell him to shove it, which is pretty much what I did tell him. The army men didn't have that option. They were at the mercy of the chain of command, at the very top link of which was the general who was determined to get rid of the Green Berets once and for all.

A few days after I got to Vietnam I received a note smuggled out of the Long Bin jail. It was from the six Green Beret officers who were being held there. This is how the note ended: ". . . we are . . . convinced that we are on the short end of a personal vendetta by a very powerful and determined man. Events so far have borne out this theory."

The "powerful and determined man" was of course General Abrams. To understand Abrams's attitude, let me tell you a bit about the Green Berets, as I got to know them.

The typical Green Beret outfit was notable for its lack of spit and polish and its disregard for military ritual so dear to the hearts of many general officers. And the Berets were an elite organization exempt from much army discipline. They lived day and night with imminent death. They learned to cope with the brutality and the unreality that marked the Vietnam of that period. If on occasion they were trigger-happy it was because they had learned that they would live and die by the law of the jungle hell into which they had been thrown.

The Berets were not men who killed for the mere pleasure of killing. In fact, they prided themselves on their professionalism. I believed then and I believe now that they would no more have killed an unarmed Vietnamese woman or child than a member of their own family. Colonel Rheault, commanding officer of the Berets in Vietnam, was as decent a human being as I have ever met. It was one of the great tragedies of the Green Beret case that his military career, which meant the world to him, was destroyed because of it.

The Green Berets, as a group, were colorful, adventurous soldiers. Most of them were uncomplicated extroverts whose off hours were filled with high-spirited pursuits. This was less true of the intelligence officers who were my clients. But they too possessed a share of the Green Beret esprit.

Thai Khac Chuyen, whom the Berets were accused of murdering, was the interpreter and guide for an intelligence-gathering unit operating out of Nha Trang, headquarters of the Special Forces group. Chuyen had been recruited by Sergeant First Class Alvin I. Smith, Jr. of Naples, Florida.

Smith accidentally uncovered solid evidence that Chuyen was betraying Green Beret patrols to the North Vietnamese. Smith gave him a lie detector test and an injection of Pentothal, the truth serum. Both indicated strongly that Chuyen was a double agent who had already done much harm and would inevitably cause more if given the opportunity.

Informed by Smith of the test results, his superiors got in touch at once with their CIA counterparts in Nha Trang because the two worked closely together in intelligence gathering. The CIA agent didn't think twice about this problem.

"Kill him," he said.

"But how about your Saigon people?" the Berets asked. "Will they go along?"

"Don't worry about Saigon," the CIA man replied. "The guy there has handled 250 political killings. What's one more?"

But the Green Berets were still uneasy. Summary executions just weren't their cup of tea. So they waited for a go-ahead from the CIA. But a deep silence had set in there. As one Green Beret officer said bitterly afterwards: "Those guys are great poker players. They suck you in and then give you the zinger."

Three days passed and the Green Berets were still waiting for definite word. At last, after trying repeatedly to reach the

CIA people, they decided they were being given a tacit okay and that the safety of the whole outfit demanded that they get rid of Chuyen at once. Chuyen was given a shot of morphine, put in a small boat and taken out into Nha Trang Bay. There, the Army charged, Captain Marasco put a .22 caliber bullet through his head. Then the body was loaded with chains and thrown into the bay—200 feet deep at that point.

The very next day—as if they had been waiting for the Green Berets to pass the point of no return—the CIA finally spoke up. They told the Berets to return Chuyen to duty because he represented the "highest moral and flap potential."

The stunned Green Berets, realizing they had been mouse-trapped, hemmed and hawed and then said the first thing that came to mind: Chuyen was on a sensitive mission and could not be contacted. That, they thought, took care of that.

It didn't. Sergeant Smith, who felt a special responsibility for Chuyen as a man he recruited, now panicked. He turned himself in at CIA headquarters in Nha Trang and pleaded for protection against his Green Beret associates. They had killed Chuyen, he said, and he was probably marked for a similar fate because he recruited the double agent and had stood up for him.

Now the fat was in the fire. The Nha Trang CIA sped the word to their brass in Saigon, and they in turn rushed to General Abrams with the story. Abrams, as already suggested, had utter contempt for the Green Berets, regarding them as irresponsible glory hunters who only got in the way of real soldiers. (Besides, they wore funny clothes.) He immediately put two top investigators on the case. They went to work with enthusiasm. A few threats and a little cajolery and they had enough to make Abrams see red.

Minutes later he had Colonel Rheault on the phone and put it to him bluntly: "Did your men kill Chuyen? Yes or no."

Taken off guard, Rheault floundered. He repeated the made-up story that Chuyen was off on a secret mission. Later he said that he feared that someone was listening in. Perhaps so. But I suspect that it was concern for his men that pressured him into doing something that was completely foreign to his nature: concealing facts. Actually, all he succeeded in doing was to confirm Abrams's low opinion of the Green Berets.

Like most military posts, Saigon had a very effective grapevine. Within hours, everyone down to the newest recruit knew that an apopleptic Abrams had told his people to "go in there and clean out those bastards." From then on things moved very fast, as they usually do in armies when the man at the top passes on the word.

Colonel Rheault was picked up and put into a house trailer in the Long Binh stockade. The six lower-ranking officers were thrown into stifling, maximum-security, five-by-seven-foot cells. CWO Boyd and Sergeant Smith were separated from the others because the prosecutors had plans for them.

Jailers—military or civilian—have an unfailing instinct for the kind of treatment to accord prisoners. If the prosecutor hates the prisoner's guts, you may be sure that the guard will miraculously get the message. That is why everywhere in the world you will see some defendants practically handed the keys to the jail while others are treated like lepers. The Green Beret officers definitely were not given the keys to the jail.

My reputation as a troublemaker apparently preceded me to Saigon, because the day I got there the Army hastily stopped playing Spanish Inquisition. They let the officers out of their cells and gave them tolerable lodgings.

In a way, I was sorry about this because I was primed to release a blast that would have spoiled Abrams's dinner for him. I have a deep-seated dislike for officious bureaucrats and I enjoy nothing better than to catch them at their arrogant little games and take them down a peg or two.

In one way or another, I managed to convey to most of Saigon that I was not a member of the Abrams Fan Club. Harry Truman is reported to have said about General Douglas MacArthur, whom he dismissed from command for insubordination: "I fired him because he wouldn't respect the authority of the President. I didn't fire him because he was a dumb son-of-a-bitch, although he was, but that's not against the law for generals. If it was, half to three quarters of them would be in jail."

I had no reason to believe that Truman would have counted Abrams among those suitable for incarceration. But I just didn't like the way the general was throwing his substantial weight around at the expense of my clients.

My first task was to represent my clients at the Article 32 investigation hearing, which is the equivalent of a preliminary hearing in a civilian court. The hearing went very well for us at a cost of about ten pounds off my already spare frame. The hearing room was the chapel at Long Binh, where the mercury never went below 100 during the time I was there. And no air conditioning.

I tried to make the courtroom even hotter for the CIA agents and their military counterparts. During cross examination, they must have lost a bit more poundage than I did. In any event, I learned later that Abrams's people had reported to him that I had wrecked their case.

Even though he was on the other side, I felt a bit sorry for one CIA man. Every time I shot an embarrassing question at him, he had to reply: "I'm sorry, sir, I cannot answer your question. I've been ordered by my superiors to invoke executive immunity under the U.S. Code. We are an agency of the executive branch of the government and we invoke executive immunity."

Since Watergate, this business of executive immunity has fallen into the disfavor it deserves. But at that time the military and its friends thought it was the greatest thing since apple pie. In their delight with this new toy they had been handed, they overlooked the devastating effect it was having on their case. They would have been much better advised to forget their precious immunity and to level with Colonel Harold Seaman, the investigative officer who was presiding. Seaman was a sensible man, not a lawyer (I don't mean to imply that the two are mutually exclusive) and he obviously found this immunity ploy irksome.

The CIA agent had been placed in a most difficult position

by his superiors. Perhaps it was not kind, but I had to point up
the fact that we were dealing with human beings, not with
some abstract problem of evidence.

"We're here in an American court of military justice," I said
to the agent, "and all of us, you and I and all of these officers
sitting here, are interested in one great thing, and that is to
learn the truth. Is this not so?"

The reply of course had to be yes.

"You'll agree with me, will you not," I went on, "that these
questions I'm putting to you now, these questions that you
decline to answer, would shed a great deal of light on the
accusations against these officers. Don't you think, under the
principles of basic justice, that the truth should be heard and
tested right here in this courtroom and that you should tell us
that truth and not hide behind the immunity you invoke?"

He left the room a weary and unhappy man. But my point
was made. To reinforce the point, I said to Colonel Seaman:
"The prosecution can't have it both ways. Either lay all the
evidence on the table and make it available to us so that we can
examine and cross-examine, or forget the case. And I suggest
you forget the case."

Everything looked good and I went back to New York
feeling quite pleased. I was aware that Secretary of the Army
Stanley Resor was in Saigon talking with Abrams, and I was
sure he was asking some searching questions about the Green
Beret case. As it turned out, the first item on Resor's agenda
was getting American troops out of Vietnam. As I later heard
the story, Abrams resented Resor's advising him to drop the
Green Beret case as quickly as possible.

"I'll get the troops out for you without blowing the war,"
Abrams is said to have shouted at Resor, "but you leave the
Berets to me."

Abrams apparently had his way. Soon, his underlings gloat-
ingly announced that the Berets would be court-martialed on
charges of murder. When I heard what Abrams was up to, I
thought of the Roman aphorism: "Whom the gods would
destroy they first make mad."

Back I went to Vietnam. At the airport I was met by several

wonderful young Green Berets, one of them carrying a sign in Vietnamese.

"Know what it says?" he asked me.

When I shook my head no, he told me: "It says 'Get Abrams.' "

I called together the military lawyers who were my co-counsel and said: "It seems we're taking on not only the top brass here in Vietnam but also the Secretary of the Army and the Secretary of Defense. And probably President Nixon, as well. I know you're all lawyers first and Army officers second, so let's forget all about rank."

Nobody has ever accused me of being afraid of a cliché, so it's quite possible that I added that the bigger they come the harder they fall.

Right then and there we set about "getting" Abrams. And Abrams, it quickly became obvious, had the same intention towards us. No more courtesies, no more friendly drinking sessions with the opposition. Fraternizing was definitely out. Worse, we were given no transportation, no office, no type-writers, no typists. Our mail and phone calls, even our memos to each other, were monitored by a Watergate-type plumbers squad. They weren't especially skillful plumbers but they did their best to annoy.

When I needed to read the transcripts of the Article 32 hearing in order to refresh my recollection, they made it as difficult and uncomfortable as possible. At one point, I said to Major Linsky, who was sharing a miserable hovel with two fellow officers, "Where are we supposed to read these tran-scripts? Sitting out under the broiling sun, in the dust?" Abrams clearly was not anxious to be known as a nice guy.

But even more troubling than this harassment was a new prosecution maneuver. The Army, preying on the natural fears of CWO Boyle and Sergeant Smith, promised them immunity from prosecution. The idea, of course, was to have them testify that they had witnessed the murder, thus proving the *corpus delicti*, that is the body of the crime. Since Chuyen's body couldn't be produced, this was important for the pros-ecution's case. In a trial with a number of defendants you can be sure that one or more will jump on the prosecution's bandwagon. It was something to worry about.

We decided that if they wanted to play rough, we would oblige them. Our initial move was to flood the prosecution with legal motions. The Army brass, accustomed to the short, relaxed headquarters day that was merely a prelude to the serious drinking of the evening, was obviously thrown off balance.

First, we filed a motion that Colonel Rheault and the others be permitted to hold a press conference. Since the prosecution, we pointed out, had held such a conference—at which they had done everything possible to blacken our clients' characters—we felt that, in all fairness, we should have one in order to reply in kind. The motion was promptly denied but I observed that our adversaries looked a bit jumpy.

Next, we made a motion for logistical support comparable to the prosecution's. We asked for a telephone exchange connecting defense counsels' rooms and defendants' rooms, so that we could talk freely with our clients.

Then came the clincher. The reason we needed all this at once, we mentioned casually, was that F. Lee Bailey and Edward Bennett Williams were joining the defense.

Now the prosecutors were clearly jittery. They may have thought that they could contain Rothblatt by cutting off his comforts, conveniences, and communications, but they did not relish the prospect of Bailey and Williams also raising hell with them, which they very well know how to do.

To prepare for our distinguished colleagues and for our own needs, we asked for an air-conditioned sedan, photograph equipment, tape recorders, post exchange and officers' mess privileges, and a secretary for each civilian counsel. All summarily denied.

In the end, we got the operating support we needed from the press. The TV networks, the wire services, and the newspapers, for which we were providing colorful copy day after day, proved to be generous friends. As a result, all of Abrams's petty persecutions were no more effective against us than his military "genius" was against the North Vietnamese and the Viet Cong.

Members of the media were our natural allies, since they were thoroughly fed up with the military briefings that glorified the top brass and covered up the meager results of their efforts. I am sure that Abrams deeply regretted that he could not court-martial the less-than-admiring reporters.

As I got to know them, I developed a genuine respect for those covering the war. Their superiority in brains, personality, and culture over the Army brass was so marked as to be embarrassing. But the brass was too wrapped up in self-esteem to notice.

The Army had gone all out to increase the "body count," sometimes for its own reassurance and sometimes out of a mistaken notion that reporting mountains of enemy corpses would somehow placate the American public and the politicians who controlled the purse strings. All that this "body count" nonsense succeeded in doing was to tarnish the image of the American combat soldier.

Most of the junior officers I met—roughly up to the rank of captain—were able, attractive people. But for some reason, high rank seemed to produce a Colonel Blimp mentality that would have been funny if it had not been so tragic for our country and for the soldiers in the field. More than once I found myself thinking that if I had a son who was killed by the eternal bungling, I would not be responsible for my actions.

Now that we had support from our media friends, it was time for our most dramatic motion. This was nothing less than a formal request to the President of the United States that, as commander-in-chief of the armed forces, he end the Green Beret case, or failing this, order a new Article 32 hearing with himself as presiding officer—in order to avoid the command influence exerted by General Abrams.

We also bore down hard on the executive immunity claimed by the CIA in order to sidestep embarrassing questions. This claim, we maintained, wasn't worth a damn without his, the president's, specific approval.

We wound up with a flourish: "It's basic to any sense of democratic justice that the policeman cannot be policeman, judge and jury all rolled up into one. We want you, Mr. President, to be the judge, if you won't dismiss the charges."

This may sound like so much empty oratory. Nevertheless, I have learned that politicians—and presidents must be master politicians—are quick to recognize a point that appeals to their countrymen. In the plight of the Green Berets, we felt that we had an emotional issue that would get the sympathy of the American people.

Meanwhile, the prosecutor was not about to throw in his hand. In fact, he was convinced that he had an ace in the hole in the person of CWO Boyle. Using the divide-and-conquer technique, the prosecutor had continued wooing Ed Boyle after giving him immunity. This is often an effective tactic, since a defendant who has been living in fear of a long prison term is naturally ecstatic when the threat is lifted. I have seen defendants so overwhelmed by the "generosity" of the prosecutor that they regard him as a human god and ignore all former ties and loyalties.

My own feeling was that the prosecutor was kidding himself. Ed, of course, was vastly relieved at having been granted immunity. But after the initial euphoria, he began to realize that he could not rat on his comrades. I had a friendly chat with Boyle and found that he was deeply grateful to the prosecutor and terrified of Abrams. All the same he could not bring himself to speak out firmly against his buddies.

At this strategic moment, James Sterba, *The New York Times'* tireless and perceptive correspondent in Vietnam, played a key role. Sterba's interest was in getting a story, not in helping the defendants. As it turned out, he did both.

I set up an interview for Sterba with Boyle. The newspaperman quickly realized that Boyle was not going to testify as the Army hoped he would.

On September 27, I left for the United States, since I had a case to try in San Francisco. On that very day, Sterba's story ran in the *Times.* Never before was the power of the press more dramatically demonstrated to me.

Two days later, I was in the midst of cross-examining a witness when a reporter burst into the courtroom with the great news. The President had just announced that the case against the Green Berets was being dropped.

General Creighton Abrams, Jr., commanding general of the U.S. Army in Vietnam, was left high and dry.

The Green Berets were freed.

Later, when I was involved with the Watergate case and had my own grievances against Richard Nixon, I still felt that he had handled the Green Beret mess wisely and humanely. Obviously, he made the decision himself, without the help of the "brilliant" advisors who later helped pitch him into the Big Muddy of Watergate.

Once the case had tumbled down about the Army's ears, and all the briefing officers and their retinues had fled to the dim recesses of the headquarters bars, the Army rushed out a statement that gave no hint of the all-out campaign it had mounted to convict the Green Berets. Here is a short selection from the Army's psalm-singing:

> The Central Intelligence Agency, though not directly involved in the alleged incident, determined that in the interest of national security it would not make available any of its personnel as witnesses in connection with the pending trials in Vietnam of Army personnel assigned to the 5th Special Forces group . . . The Secretary of the Army decided that under the circumstances the defendants could not receive a fair trial. On September 29, 1969 he directed that all charges be dismissed immediately . . . It would be unjust to assess the culpability of any individual involved in this matter without affording him an opportunity to present his defense in a full and fair trial. Under our system of jurisprudence, every man accused of wrong-doing is presumed to be innocent until he is proved guilty . . . The determination of guilt may be made only by a court which has access to all information with respect to the alleged offense.

Holy, holy.

More than a year after the "end" of the war in Vietnam, the Green Berets whom Abrams had tried so hard to destroy were engaged in one of their typically dangerous missions. Based in

Thailand, they were assigned to special teams searching for the remains of Americans missing, in some cases, for almost ten years. In the process, they were suffering casualties from communists who didn't know or didn't care that the war was over. But though the Green Berets were still dodging grenades and bullets, General Abrams had already left Vietnam and eventually retired.

THREE

The Bizarre Matzner Story

I'VE ALREADY suggested that the weird and the unexpected fascinate me. But just about the time I think I've seen everything, along comes a case so bizarre and so frustrating that I long for a period of quiet sanity. Such a case was the Matzner murder mystery. The two trials featured a parade of psychopathic witnesses, convicted criminals offering fanciful testimony, and an assortment of court and police officials whose conduct strained credulity.

One remarkable result of the travesty was that Passaic County in New Jersey awarded my client, Police Sergeant John De Groot, $25,000, when it dropped its case against him! But let's back up.

Harold Matzner had been charged with murder. He retained my good friend F. Lee Bailey for his defense. As the case progressed, Lee became increasingly exasperated with the irresponsible antics of the prosecution. Finally, he exploded in a letter to the governor of New Jersey and to every local legislator and congressman. A typical paragraph: "Should this trial proceed as presently planned, the stench arising from it will hold the state of New Jersey up to ridicule such as beset no organ of government since the abolition of the Star Chamber."

Promptly on receipt of the letter the New Jersey Supreme Court removed Bailey from the case. The court could do this because Lee was not a member of the New Jersey bar. He had been given special permission to appear as an out-of-state attorney.

To digress a bit further, it was not always this way in New Jersey. Some years back, the state came up with a remarkable judicial system called the "number one legal miracle of the century." The miracle was largely the doing of one great man—New Jersey's chief justice, the late Arthur T. Vanderbilt. He reorganized the state's archaic court system and abolished century-old abuses that had made justice a mockery. "It is our duty not only to be just but to be known to be just," he said, and the majority of lawyers throughout the land cheered at his words. Some of the good that Vanderbilt had accomplished unfortunately seems to have been buried with him.

Ironically, if Lee had been less honest and fearless, he would have kept his mouth shut, won his case, collected a big fee, and been a local hero. But he did not want to take part in an enormous boondoggle. He knew that the case would drag on and on, that his client would have to pay enormous fees. And there was no real challenge for him in knocking down the assemblage of crooks and psychos the state had dredged up to testify against Matzner.

With Lee out, I stepped in to hold the fort. It wasn't long before I began to share Lee's rage. The Matzner case, I felt, would be comical if it were not so terrifying an example of official folly and arrogance.

I remember thinking as I looked on in horror that the only logical explanation of the goings-on was that the prosecutor had been watching too much television. On TV, crimes are so simple. There's a murder, then another murder. There's some counterfeiting going on (in an abandoned warehouse down by the river with good facilities for gunfire, bale-toppling and a chase.) Obviously, the counterfeiters murdered the two because they knew too much. But the brilliant, dogged D.A. isn't fooled. He tracks down some witnesses, the chief counterfeiter is killed by a heavy bale that falls on his head, the other culprits are speedily rounded up, and the D.A. smiles modestly as the commercial comes on.

That isn't the way the Matzner case turned out.

In Clifton, New Jersey, on February 24, 1966, Judy Kavanaugh, twenty-one, married to twenty-four-year-old Paul Kavanaugh, was reported missing by her husband.

A short time afterwards, her car was discovered on fire in an isolated area of Newark. A couple of weeks later, her partially nude body was found in a gully near her home. At the autopsy, two bullets were found in her head, and there was an indication that she had been strangled.

Police must lead unusually unhappy home lives, because whenever a wife is found murdered, they immediately pounce on the husband. Having no evidence against Kavanaugh, however, they did the next best thing. They locked him up on $10,000 bail as a material witness.

Kavanaugh would have stayed in jail except for one thing: he was a newspaper deliverer for Matzner Publications, a modestly prosperous chain. Harold Matzner, then twenty-eight, who ran the business for his father, was a short, stocky man with an unfortunate temper. He put up bail for Kavanaugh and opened his home to him.

If this sounds odd for an employer and an employee, it should be kept in mind that these were small-town folks, both young, both shocked by the tragedy. But now the police had two suspects. After all, why should Matzner be so nice to Kavanaugh?

Not far away, in Paterson, there lived one of the country's less desirable citizens, one Gabriel De Franco, a numbers-racket controller for the Mob.

He was making plenty—about $1,500 a week—but he wanted more. He got it by short-changing his bosses, a procedure not recommended for one in his position. The bosses found out, but were uncharacteristically lenient. They cut off his income but left his head intact.

De Franco missed his steady salary, especially since he had three dependents—a racehorse and two young punks, John and Frank Shea, his intimate companions.

As it happened, a West Coast counterfeiter, one Andy King, turned up at this critical juncture with a bale of reasonably passable bills. De Franco and the Sheas gratefully agreed to help him unload the fake bills. In less than a month De Franco, King, the Sheas and a few other stupid hoods were behind bars for passing counterfeit money.

But what does all this have to do with Matzner? Please bear with me. All will soon be clear.

De Franco was released on unusually low bail for a man of his achievements. This was convenient for him but worrisome for the Mob. Was there some deal cooking with the government? Was De Franco blowing the whistle on the Mob?

If there was such a deal it died on October 6, 1966, along with De Franco. Answering a knock on the door of his apartment, De Franco had his throat cut from ear to ear, quickly, neatly and professionally.

Now the plot thickens. Searching De Franco's apartment after the murder, what do the police find but Matzner's telephone number. Obviously incriminating, they feel. To further complicate the picture, they find a racetrack pass, made out to Matzner, in De Franco's car.

Matzner's explanation: De Franco, an avid moonlighter, had been a valuable source of underworld news stories. Very good for circulation. Matzner had paid him in cash, occasional loans, and the use of the track pass. Not very bright of him, but certainly not a unique arrangement between a newspaperman and his tipsters.

Now enter the first two of a series of eager-beaver assistant prosecutors, Robert Kessler and Charles Carroll.

Matzner, they realized happily, had figured in the Kavanaugh case and here he was again in another murder investigation! Clearly, this was beyond coincidence.

Without wasting a moment, Kessler and Carroll set to work. The prosecutor's office had been dozing over the Kavanaugh case for months. But no longer. Kessler and Carroll speedily had Paul Kavanaugh indicted for his wife's murder and Harold Matzner for obstructing justice.

They just *knew* that the De Franco case was somehow tied in with the Kavanaugh murder, and now they were going to smoke out the perpetrators. Just like on TV.

Now let's take a look at the man in charge of investigating both murders, pudgy Joe Muccio.

Twenty years earlier, Muccio had been mayor of West Paterson. This was during the heyday of Joe Adonis and Willie Moretti. These two had enjoyed a lucrative and undisturbed gambling operation there until the Feds put them out of business.

Muccio then left the scene of his glory and got himself a job as an attendant in court. Finally, he wound up as investigator to the Passaic County prosecutor. He had considerable political clout and enjoyed various emoluments which enabled him to live in style.

One of the witnesses turned up by Muccio was Mrs. Jacqueline Natoli, a thirty-one-year-old hardened offender specializing in fraud. She was diagnosed as "severely neurotic, with many sociopathic features." Obviously, a perfect witness.

Finding herself in trouble, with prison looming because of a recent swindle, she was delighted to tell Muccio what he wanted to hear. Of course, she knew all about the De Franco and Kavanaugh murders.

Then followed one of the weirder incidents in a long series of weird incidents. Acting on some mysterious impulse, Muccio showed Mrs. Natoli a pornographic movie and then asked her whether she recognized Matzner and Kavanaugh as two of the actors.

It's interesting to imagine Mrs. Natoli's astonishment at the strange goings-on. But, cooperative witness that she was, she said yes, that was them all right. In fact, she had been there when the film was made. And, she added in one of her wild flights of fancy, the female lead was a woman "disguised as Judy Kavanaugh." Even Muccio must have looked puzzled by this.

Muccio next dug up another pair of convenient witnesses—the Shea brothers, out on bail in the counterfeiting case.

Since Frank was also facing a drug charge in New York, he proved even more cooperative than Mrs. Natoli. De Franco told him that he helped Matzner dispose of Judy's body, he said.

Brother John, facing a burglary charge in Greenburgh, New York, was equally anxious to do his bit for justice. He told Muccio that he had seen Matzner order one of De Franco's men to burn Judy's car.

At this point, even as the stage was being set for the trial, the scenery began to fall apart. First to collapse was the pornography bit. This was supposed to convey not only the moral depravity of Matzner and Kavanaugh but also to supply some kind of motive for the murder. A film expert found that no one in the movie could be identified. Then a dirty-film buff recognized the movie as an oldie having no connection with Matzner, Kavanaugh, or anyone known to either of them.

Other parts of the prosecution began to disintegrate, too. Matzner produced proof that he was in Chicago at a press convention the night Kavanaugh's wife was killed. He presented signed restaurant receipts and a hotel registration card. The prosecution's own handwriting expert confirmed that the signatures were genuine.

About this time, too, the prosecution's claim that somehow the fake money led to Judy's death also fell apart. It was definitely shown that the bogus bills were printed *after* she was killed.

Detective Sergeant John De Groot, who investigated the Kavanaugh murder in Clifton, decided that he had had enough. He could no longer go along with Muccio's absurd theories. In the tortuous thought processes of the prosecution, this made him a prime suspect in the "related" De Franco killing, as he was shortly to discover.

The prosecutors, meanwhile, were beginning to realize that they had the weakest pair of cases in the history of jurisprudence. Undaunted, they came up with still another convict from their jails to serve justice as their new star witness.

Enter Edward Lenney, serving a long term for robbery and sporting a formidable criminal record. Muccio treated him like visiting royalty, showing him the greatest time a prisoner in the custody of a prosecutor ever had.

In a previous attempt to curry favor, Lenney claimed that he killed De Franco, at the personal request of Johnny Ventura, a Paterson hood. But since Muccio preferred it another way, he had no trouble switching to Harold Matzner and Sergeant De Groot as the killers.

So, on such evidence, were Matzner and De Groot indicted for murder. That must have been the most cooperative grand jury that ever sat.

But now the props began to topple all over the set. Lenney, it turned out, had been tending bar some 200 miles away—in Baltimore—the night De Franco was murdered. Nine witnesses had seen Lenney in the bar.

Not surprisingly, Prosecutor John Thevos suddenly felt ill and asked the New Jersey attorney general to assign outside lawyers to prosecute the case. James Dowd and Richard McGlynn were brought in—just in time to hear Lenney confess that nothing he had said about the case was even remotely true.

Dowd asked Thevos to throw out the case. When he refused, Dowd and McGlynn wisely jumped ship.

Incredibly, preparations to try the case went on. The authorities were aware by now that they were facing a multimillion-dollar damage suit if they admitted their fantastic errors. They decided to fight to the last ditch, even though they had no ammunition to fight with.

Now came Lee Bailey's famous letter. In addition to the part I have already quoted, it included the comment: "I have never in any state or Federal court seen such abuses of justice, legal ethics and constitutional rights as this case has involved."

Out went Bailey. In came Rothblatt to pick up the defense. On went the state's preparation for the trial.

Muccio and his "investigators" traveled far and wide in their gallant "search for witnesses"—mostly in restaurants and bars. They entertained themselves, their friends and prospective witnesses royally at county expense.

A new special prosecutor, Matthew Boylan, came in. But the thing had become too ridiculous to go on much longer.

Mrs. Natoli, Lenney, and the Shea brothers had gone wild, what with all the free liquor, gourmet food, and accommodating female companions for the men. Adding to the gaiety was the realization that the law had become their good friend and that they could stop worrying about such inconveniences as the police, jails, and indictments.

The prosecution, meanwhile, studiously ignored logical suspects—for one, the racketeer, Johnny Ventura, first named as a Mob informer in the De Franco case.

Another suspect was a dishwasher who worked near the

Kavanaugh home, and who was believed to have known Judy. He quit his job the day after she disappeared. More important, the police found cinders in his room—similar to those found in the area where the body was found. And there were indications that he owned a gun of the same caliber as the murder weapon. Yet none of this was ever followed up!

A lot of New Jersey officials had by this time come to the conclusion that Bailey's letter was an understatement. But the prosecution had passed the point of no return. The farcical De Franco murder trial actually got under way.

When called to testify, Lenney, Mrs. Natoli, and the Sheas became hopelessly entangled in their lies. Everything they said exploded in their faces. One small example: Lenney claimed that he was with De Groot on the night of the De Franco murder. Yet he didn't know that De Groot was heavily bandaged that day, the result of an auto accident.

After additional absurd, confused, and contradictory testimony—and a straightforward defense—the jury quickly brought in a verdict of not guilty. The members of another jury, just as quickly, returned the same verdict in the Kavanaugh case, which was never solved.

And so the filthy doings came to an end after four years. Matzner was in debt, his wife ill, his reputation damaged, and his business on the brink of bankruptcy. The prosecution retreated behind closed doors, waiting for time to dull public repugnance over the sordid affair.

I am not a habitual admirer of the police. But the forty-four-year-old decorated officer, Detective Sergeant De Groot, was such an utterly decent, honest man that I deeply resented the treatment he received. It was gratifying for me to help him win the $25,000 already mentioned. It was just a token recompense for what he had been put through, but it did serve to clear his name and showed up the authorities once again for what they really were.

FOUR

Cast of Characters
The Police

For THE new lawyer engaged in criminal practice, the most important figure is the policeman. As cases grow in importance the cop's role diminishes. But he is still worth examining at close range.

The average policeman deserves our thanks and respect. Sergeant De Groot, who conducted himself so honorably in the Matzner case, is a good example. This type of cop strives to live up to his badge. He is ready to help people, to defend and protect them. He risks his life doing his duty as he sees it. He allows himself to become a prime target for criminals and psychopaths. He is honest, although he's not really convinced that it's wrong to accept small gifts from storekeepers or an occasional free meal from restaurants on his beat. Probably he tends to discount his superiors' scoldings because he's sure they are getting larger gifts.

Unfortunately, an occasional policeman weakens and ends up "on the take." Perhaps he begins by dealing himself in on the profits of gamblers, a breed he doesn't think of as real criminals. He watches them making big money without much effort or risk. He cannot resist the temptation of picking up some of the easy money constantly thrust on him. After all, he rationalizes, my wife likes nice things too—new couch covers, dinners out, even a few dollars in the bank. Eventually, such a policeman often finds himself drifting by easy stages into association with drug peddlers and other vermin.

This type of cop is a constant headache to top police officials. I remember talking about this with the late chief Inspector John J. Hennessey of the New York Police Department. I was very fond of Hennessey for his Irish wit and warmth. Some cops were becoming so greedy, I told Hennessey, that a major scandal was brewing.

"These guys are nothing more nor less than partners in crime," I said.

Hennessey sat staring blankly for a moment. Then he said, "Henry, I know all about it. Every once in a while, I'll start to bounce one of these thieves off the force and just about that time he shoots it out with some hood when he could just as well have stepped around the corner instead of putting his ass on the line."

"Then what?" I asked.

"I lose sleep. Then I call him in and congratulate the bum. He's standing there smiling and I grab him by the collar and say that if I ever catch him taking so much as an apple from a pushcart I'll have him in jail."

I had dinner with Hennessey shortly after he retired from the department to become security head of Schenley Industries. He looked ten years younger. His biggest problem, he assured me, was convincing former associates that he did not have the key to Schenley's liquor vault.

I detest and despise a third kind of policeman who, through incompetence, viciousness or self-interest, sets himself up as judge of the guilt or innocence of a defendant, and who will even commit perjury to get a conviction. Such a policeman, in the opinion of Chief Inspector Hennessey, is more dangerous than any lawbreaker.

An exaggeration? Well, imagine that you are a young fellow picked up by the police on suspicion of robbery. It seems a couple of people saw the robber running out of a drugstore. The robber had shot the proprietor during a holdup. The witnesses' descriptions fitted you. To make things worse, as a kid you once broke into that same drugstore. As a first offender you got a suspended sentence.

You are not really worried. You know you are innocent. The case against you is thin. Not that the police didn't try to beef it up a bit. They bounced you around in the upstairs detective room and they even tried to con you with hints that they would let you go home if you'd just "give them the facts for the record."

When they realized that you weren't dumb enough to fall for that one (you'd be surprised how many are), they booked you anyhow and the routine indictment followed.

So now you are in court with your lawyer, confident that the jury will realize that you are not guilty. Your lawyer is not quite so optimistic—he has met the arresting officer before.

The trial gets under way and all seems to be going well. A couple of witnesses testify that they saw someone of your general appearance leaving the store. They were some distance off and can't swear it was you. The druggist, recovered from his gunshot wound, says the robber looked like you, but he can't be sure. Fine. You wait for the judge to throw the case out.

But hold on. Here comes Detective "Framer" to the stand. He tells the jury that he advised you of your rights—that you didn't have to say anything and that you could consult a lawyer. This is true. He did. But a moment later the sweat breaks out all over you.

With a straight face he testifies that you admitted the whole thing on the way to the station house in a squad car. Then he throws in a few details that sound so convincing that no one could possibly have made them up. The jury, more or less relaxed during the early testimony, turns frozen-faced. You try to catch the detective's eye in the wild hope that he's mixed up your case with someone else's. Surely he'll realize his error? But he only stares back at you with an air of holy virtue.

So you take the stand, deny you ever confessed and swear that you are innocent. But, as the assistant district attorney reminds the jury in his summation, what possible reason could there be for the detective to lie? And, obviously, you had the best reason in the world to lie—you want to stay out of prison.

Incidentally, by taking the stand, you made it possible for the district attorney to cross-examine you about your previous conviction. The jury members' frozen faces turn positively glacial. They stay out only long enough for a quick cigarette.

Before you know it you are on your way to prison. When you get there, you will find a lot of others who claim that they too were framed. Most weren't, but a few were.

As the years go by, you ask yourself over and over again why the cop lied. Well, he could have any of a number of reasons. Perhaps he was too dumb or too lazy to find the actual holdup man. Maybe he felt you actually were the robber and decided that the end justified the means. No animal was going to get away with anything in his precinct, by God. Maybe his record of arrests hadn't been too good lately and he lived in fear of being sent back to pounding pavement in uniform.

So that's why you're in prison. You're bitter and full of hate. You promise yourself that when you get out you'll make "them" pay. When you do get out and the police catch on that they have a cop hater in the neighborhood, you'll be at the head of the line for another frameup.

Meanwhile, the robber who actually shot the druggist has gone his own way. He may even provide Detective Framer with a few more opportunities for perjury in the name of justice. But Framer's conscience doesn't bother him a bit. He just knows that he's ideally qualified to act as judge and jury. He has all the sublime confidence of the moral idiot he is.

Perhaps you think I am exaggerating. Please read this next case and then make up your mind. The facts were exactly as stated.

A man is on trial for a holdup for which he could get up to twenty-five years in prison. The victim takes the stand and positively identifies the defendant as the holdup man. "I could never forget that face in a hundred years," he testifies. The jury looks properly impressed.

The defense attorney, obviously discouraged, begins his cross-examination. "Did you ever see the defendant between the time of the holdup and the time of the trial," he asks idly.

Unexpectedly, the witness becomes flustered. The suddenly alerted lawyer presses him. Reluctantly, all the while casting fearful glances at the cops in the courtroom, the witness admits he saw the defendant once during that interval.

"Where?" asks the lawyer.

"In a squad car with detectives the day after the holdup."

"Did the detectives ask if that was the man who pulled the job?"

"Yes, they did." In a low voice.

The lawyer pauses dramatically. He knows that the next answer may well settle the case. "What did you tell them?"

"I said it wasn't the same man."

Sensation in the courtroom! The case is over and everyone knows it. The judge takes a short recess to think about it. Then he throws out the case. He calls the detectives into chambers and bawls them out for covering up vital evidence. Nobody, of course, asks whether the cops ever mentioned the discussion in the squad car. That would be bad manners.

One case that I tried made me furious with the police. It showed clearly that certain policemen will go to outrageous lengths to get a conviction. The case involved Norman Walter (Frenchy) Mayronne, a nineteen-year-old drifter and sex pervert I defended on a charge of murder in the first degree. The victim was a sixty-eight-year-old widow who had been raped and strangled in the hallway of her East Bronx apartment house.

Mayronne was introduced to the public by the New York *Daily News* when it ran a full page photo of him under the screaming headline, HE SLEW WIDOW OVER 15 CENTS. Other newspapers also ran lengthy descriptions of the "sadist-killer." It was truly a most horrible and sensational crime. And thanks to the press coverage, millions of New Yorkers were convinced that Mayronne was a degenerate killer.

The stories were based on a detailed "confession" Mayronne had given to the police and duly repeated to an assistant district attorney. No one, it seems, bothered to question whether the confession was true.

Mayronne was an ideal suspect: a homeless, psychotic youth given to perverted sex practices, well known in the neighborhood where the crime took place. Looking back, it's obvious that it was precisely because of his personality and background that Mayronne was arrested.

There was no evidence whatsoever against Mayronne, but

the conscientious detectives took care of that in the upstairs room. After a sample of their technique, he decided it would be wise to adopt every word the detectives put into his mouth.

The Mayronne case is an excellent example of how phony confessions can take on such color and detail that it is almost impossible to imagine that they are not true. But, if you keep in mind that the defendant is a mere ventriloquist's dummy, with the police serving as puppet masters, the whole thing quickly falls into place.

Take this one item: The murdered woman had been wearing a black coat. Mayronne told this to the district attorney's stenographer. If Mayronne was innocent how could he know about the black coat?

Elementary! During the eighteen hours of questioning, the police put in little helpful hints like, "Was her coat *black* or blue? Was it *black* or purple? Was it *black* or white?"

Mayronne, despite his eccentricities, was not stupid. He mastered the code quickly. Once this tacit understanding was established, every fact known to the police about the victim's dress, the scene of the crime, and the crime itself was transmitted to Mayronne. After careful rehearsals, Mayronne repeated these facts to the district attorney. (This procedure was also used in the famous Whitmore case. A black youth gave a detailed account of how he had murdered two career girls, although he had never been with them! Luckily, the real culprit was turned up years later by the efforts of journalist Selwyn Raab, much to police embarrassment.)

When I took over Mayronne's defense, he was confused and frightened because of treatment by the police. He had such fear and hatred of all authorities—including district attorneys, psychiatrists, and even court clerks—that it was impossible for me to confer with him. For a while, he remained sure that I was plotting along with the others to have him sent to Matteawan as a homicidal maniac. He watched every move I made with deep suspicion.

No cop bent on getting a suspect convicted will ever admit saying an unkind word to a suspect, much less striking him. My technique with this kind of smooth liar is simple. After he has sworn with utmost fervor that neither he nor any of his fellow officers laid a finger on the defendant, I ask him suddenly, "Well, have you ever *heard* of a police officer using force to get a confession?" In the full flow of his denials, he is as likely as not to say, "No, I haven't." Even the most credulous of jurors finds that hard to swallow. Some may even laugh in his face. In any case, he is effectively discredited.

In the Mayronne case, the police made one basic error. They were so busy getting Mayronne's confession that they neglected to follow up the numerous leads they had. In my cross-examination of the witnesses, I was able to show that the police failed to pursue their fingerprint investigation and that such a check would have cleared my client. Hearing these developments, the jury began looking at each other in disbelief.

It was significant too that the assistant district attorney who took down the confession was not called to testify. Neither, oddly enough, was the building superintendent who discovered the body.

Toward the end of the trial, Mayronne began to appear clearly as an unfortunate, miserable creature of the streets, without friends or family to help him—a most likely candidate for police suspicion.

During the trial, a Bellevue psychiatrist testified to Mayronne's bewilderment and disorientation. His words had a powerful effect on the jury.

I was surprised the jury stayed out as long as it did before bringing in a not-guilty verdict. Like most honest citizens, the jury members apparently found it hard to believe that the police could, like the cat in *Alice in Wonderland,* appoint itself judge and jury and condemn the accused to death.

Policemen tend to admire and respect solid citizens, especially those with wealth or political connections. But show certain cops a helpless suspect, preferably black or Puerto Rican, and the other side of their nature comes out.

Police regard for respectability works out nicely—for the right people. A Westchester upper-crust couple I know got a call one night from a New York precinct house; their son, a college student, had been picked up in a midtown alley as he was oiling a long "gravity" knife he had just bought.

The couple rushed into town and was greeted with deference by the police, who said they were sorry they had to take the boy in, but, after all, the knife *was* a little long and they had acted for his own protection. Then all three members of the family drove home.

If the boy had been one of our so-called "disadvantaged," I assure you that the treatment would have been quite different. At the very least he would have been asked endless questions and would have spent the night in jail. He might have been released the next day—if there were no unsolved crimes in the neighborhood at the time.

It's my opinion that Mayronne's arrest—eleven days after the murder—was largely the result of pressure on the police for results. When the boss sends along word that the public is clamoring for results—and fast—police officers get the message.

Many laymen do not realize that there are police quotas, and a consequent need for "pinches." I recall one peaceful Sunday afternoon when my phone rang at home. It was an assistant district attorney asking if I would turn in one of my clients accused of a crime. By all means, I told him, I'd take care of it first thing in the morning. He hung up.

Five minutes later he rang back. With some embarrassment, he asked if I would mind bringing my client in that very day—Sunday. Now I blew my top. I demanded to know what was the all-fired emergency. Hesitantly, the assistant district attorney explained. It was the last day of the month and the arresting officer needed one more "collar" to meet his monthly quota of eight. Any wonder, then, that there are so many unjustified arrests, in small as well as important cases?

Now and then an unusual circumstance affords the public a glimpse of the murky world of police misconduct. When the office of Daniel Ellsberg's psychiatrist was broken into, the police quickly got a "voluntary" confession out of a luckless junkie and packed him off to jail. Later, when it became known that the White House "plumbers" were responsible, there were some red faces among the police. They don't like being caught at their little game.

In a different vein, imagine the frustration of a well-meaning policeman who makes an arrest according to the book, tells the truth in court and finds that the judge doesn't believe him. In one case, I unwittingly subjected a policeman to this ordeal.

In court, the policeman told this story: He raided a shop run by my client. A search uncovered records of number payoffs, stacks of betting slips—the works. While making the arrest, the phone rang. He picked it up, listened for a moment and then snapped, "Too late. The betting window is closed."

And then, continued the policeman, the storekeeper said to him, "Why didn't you let me take the bet?"

This question struck me as very unlikely under the circumstances. "Your Honor," I said to the judge. "Is it likely that a bookie caught with betting slips hidden in his shop would ask such a question? Wouldn't he be more likely to scream his innocence—to swear that he can't imagine how the slips got there?"

The judge reflected a moment, smiled and threw the case out of court.

As we walked out of the courtroom, I said to my client, "Imagine that cop making up such a story."

"He didn't make it up," said my client. "I did ask him to let me take the bet."

FIVE

Michelle and
the Statue of Liberty

I AM AS fond of the Statue of Liberty as the next good American and I would hate to see the noble lady get blown up. Yet, I defended someone who had precisely that deed in mind.

Her name is Michelle Duclos and back in the mid-1960s she was a prominent figure on Canadian radio and television. Her program, *Profils et Caractères*, telecast on Montreal's French-language station, CFTM, was extremely popular throughout the province of Quebec.

Few who saw Michelle's dark good looks and smiling face on TV and listened to her charming voice could have suspected that she was one of the most tempestuous members of the separatist group *Rassemblement pour l'Indépendance Nationale*, an organization dedicated to Quebec's secession from Canada. This was not, at least at the time, a violent group. From time to time, the separatists would try to gain attention to their views by blowing up mailboxes. They never injured anyone but they scattered an awful lot of letters far and wide. How the Statue of Liberty became involved will be made clear shortly.

I got into the case because of a telephone call from a Canadian lawyer representing Michelle. He described the Statue of Liberty plot, and I listened with very little enthusiasm; blowing up national monuments is not the kind of action I am eager to defend. But gradually I became intrigued by the woman who managed two such disparate lives—public entertainer and private revolutionary. I wasn't entirely persuaded;

nonetheless I agreed to represent her temporarily at least. If nothing else, defending the likes of Michelle Duclos should prove to be quite an experience.

My first meeting with Michelle took place in the Women's House of Detention, an eyesore in Greenwich Village now mercifully torn down. We met for our talk in a small room. Nearby stood a woman correction officer listening intently to our conversation. Client-lawyer conversations are privileged. I said to the officer politely, "Would you mind leaving us alone? I want to have a confidential talk with my client."

"No, I won't move," she replied firmly. "Those are the rules."

I was considerably taken aback, but tired from a just-concluded trial, I took the path of least resistance. "Let's talk in French," I said to Michelle.

We proceeded to do so. Suddenly, the correction officer blurted out in French that what Michelle was saying was not true! I gave her one credit for knowing French, one demerit for revealing that knowledge, and myself two demerits for completely overlooking that possibility.

Once again, I asked the bilingual turnkey to give us some privacy. If she insisted on remaining in the room, could she please move off a bit? Once again she refused to do so, this time in resolute English. Michelle had the true Gallic temperament and refused to be intimidated by the official eavesdropper. While her jailer fumed, she described in vivid language the rampant lesbianism on her floor in the jail, and how the straight inmates were mocked and beaten.

Finally, I told the correction officer to get the warden because I had to straighten out this matter of confidentiality. When that formidable lady arrived she confirmed that jail personnel were required to sit in on attorney-client meetings. I was shocked. It was as though the Department of Correction had no knowledge of even the most elementary law principles. I made a mental note that this was virgin territory for my law books.

But more surprises were in store. When my complaint about lack of privacy was relayed to the deputy commissioner of the Department of Correction, he issued this ruling: "We have several hundred lawyers conferring every month with women prisoners and this is the first complaint of this sort we have had. We have obvious rules for obvious reasons when men confer with women. Nobody before has ever complained of them."

I was not sure what this bureaucrat's "obvious reasons" were, but I could guess. Did he really suspect that male lawyers were intent on providing other than strictly legal services to their clients?

Usually, I prefer to solve problems with diplomacy rather than muscle. So I continued to discuss the privacy issue with the correction people. All to no avail. Without further ado, I filed a writ of habeas corpus alleging that my client's rights were being violated because she was being denied effective assistance of counsel. I demanded her release from prison.

Every judge has at one time been a lawyer. I knew I would get a friendly hearing and the jailers an earful. What most policemen and jailers never get through their heads is that a person accused even of an abhorrent crime is entitled to constitutional protection.

It may seem that I am making a mountain out of a molehill, but a defendant's fate may hinge on this very matter of confidentiality. To have to discuss my defense of Michelle—there was no longer any doubt in my mind that I would represent her in court—before a jailer was tantamount to giving the other team our signals before the game. It was going to be a tough case at best. Our side was going to insist on both opponents playing by the rules.

Fortunately the assistant United States attorney in charge of the case, Stephen Kaufman, was a man of good sense. He recognized that Michelle was being done an injustice and hoped to avoid making waves. He told me that he couldn't spring Michelle from the Women's House of Detention, out of consideration for Miss Liberty and our other national monuments. Would it be inconvenient for us to use his office, he asked? He gave his word that there would be no eavesdropping, bugging, or snooping of any kind. Thank God, you can still rely on another lawyer's word—even if he is a prosecutor—and I accepted Kaufman's offer gladly.

Kaufman provided the necessary transport and a U.S. marshal to escort Michelle to his office whenever I wanted to speak with Michelle. I don't know whether they continued to allow jailers to listen in on attorney–client conversations in that prison until they tore it down. But I know they didn't whenever I was there.

Now that Michelle and I had a "secure" place to talk, she told me her story as follows.

One day she had two visitors in Montreal claiming to be members of the Black Liberation Front, a pro-Castro group. They were interested in cooperation and mutual assistance. But first they needed dynamite. One of them, twenty-eight-year-old Robert Steele Collier, was the leader of the organization. The other, Raymond Adolphus Wood, unbeknownst to Collier or to Michelle, was an undercover agent.

At the time the BLF was giving the New York City Police a big headache, not so much for any acts of violence actually committed but for the inflammatory nature of the organization's rhetoric. So the Front was under constant surveillance.

This is where Wood came in. He was a thirty-one-year-old black cop assigned to infiltrate the Front. He accomplished this very neatly. He showed up wherever the group was about to picket or demonstrate and proceeded to yell twice as loud as anyone else. The Front was not rich in volunteers and Wood was quickly accepted at his face and voice value.

The Black Liberationists considered blowing up some U.S. Army installations. Wood was careful to listen a lot and talk very little. For one thing, if he contributed to one of these schemes and it was carried out, he might be accused of entrapment.

In any case, there were serious drawbacks to the idea. The Army tended to protect these places with such devices as guard posts, barbed wire, and radar.

So the rebels hit on a bizarre alternative. They would blow up the country's most prized monuments. This, through some convoluted reasoning, would call attention to the grievances of the black population. The Statue of Liberty, the Washington Monument, and the Liberty Bell came immediately to mind. Since Miss Liberty was only a ferry ride away from Manhattan, she was put at the top of the list.

Now that the conspirators had a target to blow up, they realized that they needed dynamite. Avid readers of the exploits of other radical groups, they decided to get in touch with the Canadians who were so successful in blowing up mailboxes. No sooner said than done. Wood and Collier—a clerk in the New York Public Library—were delegated to make the trip north, which is how the two men happened to be visiting Michelle.

Michelle and the pair quickly reached a meeting of the minds. Michelle agreed to help advance the cause of black liberation by supplying enough dynamite to demolish the Statue of Liberty. As quid pro quo she asked her visitors to set aside a few hospitality suites in Harlem as hideouts for Quebec revolutionaries who might have to leave town in a hurry. No problem at all, they told her.

So, to combine business with pleasure, Michelle decided to drive down to New York with the dynamite herself. That way she could enjoy the sights of the city and perhaps take one last look at Miss Liberty while she was still standing.

Collier and Wood started back to New York and shortly afterwards Michelle placed a cardboard box—containing thirty sticks of dynamite and three blasting caps—in the trunk of a white Rambler and set off for New York. What she didn't know at the time was that the explosives, stolen from a Montreal construction site, were old and unstable. A bump in the road could conceivably have set them off, speeding the white Rambler and contents to share the fate of Canada's mailboxes.

Wood, while acting out the part of co-conspirator, had kept his superiors informed of developments. They in turn had alerted the Canadian Mounted Police. The Canadian cops followed Michelle's car to the border—more closely, no doubt, than they would have if they had known the condition of her cargo. At the border, the Canadians turned over the pursuit to the FBI, whose agents tailed the car down to the New York City line.

When Michelle got to the city, she phoned Wood to tell him that she thought she had been followed and that she was dumping the dynamite in a parking lot in the Riverdale section of the Bronx. Wood passed the word and Michelle, the Black Liberation Fronters and the dynamite were quickly collected.

The police set off the explosives where they could do no harm to the Statue of Liberty, and the revolutionaries were locked up where they likewise could do no harm. They were charged with conspiring to destroy government property, a crime that calls for a maximum penalty of ten years in prison and a $10,000 fine. Michelle was held in $100,000 bail. And that was when I entered the picture.

From the outset, I realized that Michelle was in a tough spot because of the character of Raymond Adolphus Wood, that remarkable undercover cop. He was an honest, conscientious young man and I had no wish to portray him as anything but that. If he had been less decent my job would have been easier.

Most of the undercover operatives I have known have combined an excessive greed for government money with a pathological need to betray. But Wood was not at all like that. He had been given an extremely difficult assignment and had performed brilliantly. I could only applaud when the police commissioner promoted Wood two ranks to second degree detective. Even Michelle bore Wood no grudge. In fact the more she learned about the Liberationists she was associating with, the more she came to admire Wood.

"What did the Black Liberationists tell you when you first met them?" I asked during one of our interviews.

"Oh, when they come to Montreal we go out, have some nice meals, and talk about oppressed people everywhere and how we have to show the world that we care about these people. We have to do something. For me it is a free Quebec, for them it was a free black people."

"But what does that have to do with blowing up national monuments?" I wanted to know.

She paused a bit, flickers of emotion playing on her face. "These monuments—Statue of Liberty, Liberty Bell, Washington Monument—they are all symbols of liberty, of the liberation of America from the British and of a free country, the United States, that is supposed to be a symbol of democracy for everyone. But black people are not free. All we wanted to do was make a loud explosion for equality, like in Canada."

During our talks together, I became convinced that Michelle had either been duped or, with her deep feeling for causes, had let herself believe that the Liberationists meant no harm to anyone. When she learned that they planned to dynamite the Statue of Liberty regardless of whether or not any sightseers were in or near it, she felt betrayed.

Kaufman was pleased to learn of Michelle's change of attitude toward her former associates, especially since this fit well into his plans. He realized that she would be a powerful witness to corroborate Wood's testimony. Together they would present a foolproof case against the Black Liberation Front.

I agreed that this would indeed be an effective strategy. But I wanted my client to get a fair shake for her cooperation—assuming she agreed to cooperate.

Kaufman and I agreed that Michelle would plead guilty to a reduced charge, transporting dynamite without a license, and that Kaufman would recommend to the judge that Michelle receive a suspended sentence and probation after spending the mandatory ninety days in prison. There was one other condition. Michelle was not to be extradited to Canada to face additional charges arising from the same incident. If Michelle were taken back, she might easily have done a few years in a Canadian prison, many of which I understand are even less charming than our own.

Now that the prosecution was on our side, in a manner of speaking, the next step was to persuade Michelle to testify. If she still harbored any illusions about the Front, the prosecution's strategy would be out the window and I would be back at the barricades, mustering a new line of defense.

"Michelle," I asked the next time we met, "do you still care about Collier and the others?"

"Henri, I hate them for getting me involved in their stupidity!"

So far so good, I thought. Before I could frame my next question, she blurted out, "Henri, do you think they will send me to the electric chair?"

I quickly assured her that I did not anticipate such a fate for her and that I even expected to get her freed very soon.

"I'll do anything you say. I don't want to go to the electric chair."

Michelle agreed to testify, without much enthusiasm, as a prosecution witness. I was sure she would keep her word.

Her naive fear of the electric chair was based in large part on a guilty conscience. She knew that she had disgraced herself and her movement in Canada. She feared that the Canadian government would take stern measures against her friends. In fact, one member of the group, Gilles Legault, who was among those arrested, committed suicide soon afterwards.

On May 1, 1965, Michelle appeared before U.S. District Court Judge William B. Herlands. He read the indictment, then asked, "Do you want to plead guilty?"

"Well, I am guilty," she replied, as though surprised.

"Do you throw yourself on the mercy of the court?"

"Yes, yes, I do that."

"Are you willing to take the consequences?"

"Yes."

On the stand, Michelle cooperated well with the prosecution. She was a quiet but competent witness. At the end of the trial, Collier and his two close friends received ten-year sentences.

On the appointed date, Michelle appeared before Judge Herlands for sentencing. He provisionally gave her the maximum of five years' imprisonment, the sentence to be reviewed in ninety days pending a study of her role in the affair and a probation officer's report. After ninety days, the judge would either place her on probation or make the sentence permanent.

There remained one worrisome loose end. Despite the promises made to us, there was still the possibility that Michelle might be deported. In any event, she could not stay in the United States.

Shortly after the trial, she was ordered to appear before U.S. Immigration officials. I accompanied her to that hearing. The Immigration officer demanded to know why Michelle should not be sent home. I submitted that she had paid her debt and that she should be allowed to go to France, where she could earn a living and once again be a useful citizen.

"France won't accept an undesirable like her," he said. "How do they know she won't try to blow up the Eiffel Tower?"

"Don't worry about the Eiffel Tower, or Notre Dame or the Left Bank," I assured him. "She has good friends there who will see that she stays out of trouble."

What I couldn't state openly was that the person sponsoring her was close to the De Gaulle government and not unsympathetic to the notion of an independent Quebec.

At the end of September, 1965, I drove out to John F. Kennedy International Airport and, along with two immigration officers, saw Michelle off for Paris on an Air France flight.

Over the years, I got several letters and holiday greeting cards from her. Paris obviously agreed with her. There she acquired a husband and two children. They remained in Paris for a few years. Then, when the danger of indictment for past sins was past, they moved to Quebec.

Recently, I spoke with Michelle. She was passing through New York on her way to the French Caribbean island of Martinique. She was in excellent spirits. The lack of a revolution has not created a void in her life. And the good citizens of Canada need fear no longer for their mailboxes.

SIX

Back to the Bush

ITHOUGHT I had seen the last of Vietnam but it turned out that I was mistaken. Six months after the Green Beret case I was back, wondering whether I might not have been wiser to study dentistry. It happened this way.

One day I got a call from Saigon. It was Captain John Hart, who had worked with me on the Beret case, sharing all the frustrations and the final triumph. It was good to hear his voice. As he spoke I could picture him—a big, hearty man, full of self-confidence, always ready to battle against the odds. He would have made an outstanding combat soldier.

How would I like to defend two soldiers accused of killing a Vietnamese man, he wanted to know. Names, Lieutenant James Duffy and Sergeant John Lanasa.

Here we go again, I thought. But I knew I couldn't resist. Army justice fascinated me. And, I suspect, I was a trifle bored with the mindless rapes, murders, and assorted larcenies I was defending. I also liked the Vietnamese, a gentle people who didn't deserve what was happening to them.

So I told Hart that I would get to Vietnam as soon as I could. Meanwhile, he and his co-counsel, Captain Thomas B. Thomsen, should conduct the all-important interviews of potential defense and prosecution witnesses.

When F. Lee Bailey and Melvin Belli heard that I was about to return to Saigon, they suggested that I stop off at Frankfurt, Germany, to attend a symposium on military law with them. They assured me that the stopover would help sharpen my legal tools for the joust to come with the military. Besides, Frankfurt has great beer.

I agreed and was very glad that I did. After you have spent a

few hours with Bailey and Belli, your morale soars. Neither of
them ever considers the possibility of defeat. Their confidence is contagious. Later on, during the trial, when the going
was rough, I had the eerie feeling that they were there with
me, suggesting the next move.

Hart and Thomsen were on hand with a staff car when I
landed. We went to the Caravelle Hotel, where I was greeted
as a regular customer. Remembering the climate, I changed
into a correspondent's Bao Chi suit and promptly ordered
seven more of the same from a tailor.

I also remembered the key role the press had played in the
Green Beret case, so I yielded without a struggle to requests
for interviews. This time I wanted the Army to know that we
were not going to pull any punches. This is what I told the
press:

"The Army brings men to Vietnam to fight, and the only
way the commanders can show whether or not the troops are
doing their jobs properly is by body count. We're going to
prove that the U.S. Command, by its policy of body count, in
effect is ordering officers like Jim Duffy to kill in any way they
see fit. We're going to challenge the Army on its conduct of the
war in relation to body count. We're going to subpoena everyone, from General Abrams right on down the line."

Sounds as though I was leaning pretty heavily on a body-
count defense, doesn't it? Let me tell you the details of the case
and you'll see why.

On September 4, 1969, 1st. Lieutenant James Brian Duffy,
a twenty-three-year-old gung-ho platoon commander of the
Second Battalion (Mechanized) 47th Infantry, from Clare-
mont, California, was on a night ambush patrol in the known
Communist stronghold of Phuoc Tan Hung. En route to the
ambush site, Duffy and his men came across a rice farmer's
shack, or hootch. No American G.I. in Vietnam ever passed a
hootch without peeking into it, usually through his gun sights.
This was not mere curiosity. Soldiers who ignored these
harmless-looking shacks had been known to receive a bullet in
the back from a Russian MK–1 after passing by.

Accordingly, Duffy's platoon made a routine search and

found a Vietnamese hiding in a makeshift bunker under the hootch. The platoon members considered this an unfriendly tactic and dragged the man, who was in his twenties, up for questioning.

The questioning was handled by the platoon's scout, Nguyen Duc. Duc was a former Viet Cong who was driven by all the fervor of a convert. The prisoner said his name was Do Van Man, and produced papers to show that he was an ARVN (South Vietnamese Army) private. He added that he had not enjoyed military life and had deserted his unit.

Duffy's group noticed what appeared to be recent wounds on the prisoner's body. Under vigorous questioning, he agreed that his wounds resulted from a fire fight. Since the wounds had clearly been sustained after the prisoner said he deserted the Vietnamese Army, it seemed to follow that he had been fighting as a Viet Cong. Nevertheless, the man insisted that he was not a Viet Cong. Duc continued to press him and finally the fellow made a fatal error. He admitted that at one time he had tried to join the VC but they had turned him down. This sounded very unlikely, since the belief was that anyone who could breathe and stand up was eligible.

Finally, Duc told Duffy that he was confident the prisoner was a VC. Since this coincided with his own opinion, Duffy ordered the man tied to a water-buffalo stake for the night.

Duffy then radioed his company commander, Captain Howard D. Turner, reported the capture, and asked for instructions. (Despite the everlasting chatter in Vietnam about the need for initiative and exercise of individual judgment, it seemed to me everyone spent most of his waking hours seeking instructions.) Turner told Duffy, as expected, to hold on to the prisoner until morning. To give the captain time to get instructions?

During the night the platoon whiled away the time in conversation, although the drift of their remarks boded ill for the prisoner. It seemed that headquarters had been releasing detainees even though the front-line troops bringing them in were sure they were Viet Cong. This was unnerving for the G.I.s who felt, perhaps with some justification, that one of the released might one day pull the trigger that could qualify an American for Arlington National Cemetery.

One of those arguing most forcefully for eliminating the prisoner was Sergeant John F. (Cowboy) Lanasa, the closest member of the platoon to Duffy. The two had been together in many Mekong Delta skirmishes. Both had recently been awarded their second Bronze Star for valor.

Lanasa, a former rodeo rider, son of a Baton Rouge surgeon, suggested that they finish off the prisoner Western-style, by stringing him up on a tree. Duffy vetoed this as over-picturesque for the setting, but he said that Lanasa could shoot the suspect in the morning.

Not everyone saw eye to eye with Duffy and Lanasa. Sergeant Joseph Loren, the platoon medic, and Staff Sergeant William Russell, the platoon sergeant, both objected strongly. Duffy stood his ground. "I'm not going to send him to battalion to be let go like the others," he insisted. "I'm going to have him shot and Cowboy is going to do it."

Observing the military amenities peculiar to the time and place, Russell said to Duffy, "Sir, you've got to be shitting!"

Next morning, Russell called Duffy aside and said, "Sir, even after what we talked about last night, are you still going to have that man shot?"

"Roger that," said Duffy and he walked off to wake Lanasa. "Cowboy," he said, "you can go and do what you want with the prisoner."

Lanasa rounded up three men to go with him, one of them Specialist Fourth Class Curtis M. Wilson. According to Wilson, they took Do Van Man to a wooded area a couple of hundred yards away from the shack and tied him to a tree. Lanasa raised his rifle, aimed it and squeezed the trigger.

"The weapon malfunctioned," Wilson said. "Cowboy cleared the rifle and waited for the prisoner to lift his head again. When he did, Cowboy let him have it with a single round. Then we opened up. I shot the man three times. He was all messed up . . . brains hanging out the back of his head."

When Lanasa and his firing squad returned, Duffy calmly

finished his breakfast. Then he radioed Captain Turner and told him that the prisoner had been shot while trying to escape.

Duffy later claimed that "shot while trying to escape" was a code meaning that the prisoner had been executed and that Turner knew what he meant. Turner emphatically denied it.

And there the ugly incident would have rested except for a letter that medic Loren wrote to his mother, expressing disgust at the slaying and anger with Duffy and Lanasa.

A week later, Loren was killed in action, blown up by a VC mine. His mother, in her shock and grief, feared that her son had been murdered by his own comrades because he had opposed Duffy's decision to execute the prisoner. She wrote her congressman about it and an inquiry followed. It was found that Loren had died as reported, but a finger from the grave had been pointed at Duffy and Lanasa.

The wheels of justice began grinding and Duffy and Lanasa were charged with murder and conspiracy to commit murder, under the Uniform Code of Military Justice, the same charges that had been leveled at my Green Beret clients.

Because Lanasa was still recovering from battle wounds sustained soon after the shooting of Do Van Man, Duffy went on trial first. The trial was held at II Field Force headquarters at Long Binh Post, located about twenty miles south of Saigon. Long Binh was the U.S. Command's largest military installation in Vietnam. I commuted to the sprawling complex from Saigon every day, either by taxi or in a correspondent's jeep. At least once a week, Long Binh was under enemy rocket fire and I was glad I had had the foresight to order several Bao Chi suits since I was sweating a lot, and not just from the weather.

The first few days of the trial, as always, were taken up by preliminary 39A hearings. It is at these hearings that the defense attempts to rearrange or tear down the props on the stage already set up by the Army prosecutors—by lodging motions and filing complaints, and by arguing points of law.

At length a jury of eight officers was empaneled and the prosecution opened its case before the presiding military judge, Colonel Peter Wondolowski.

Wondolowski, a big, cigar-smoking Virginian, is an able jurist with a voice very much like the late John Wayne's. He was not what I would call a defense-minded judge, but he was courteous in the Virginia tradition. There are people you meet in life whom you may not see for years. Still, you never think of them without a smile and a glow of pleasure. Wondolowski was such a person.

Despite the fine rapport between Wondolowski and me, I soon found that I was in deep trouble.

The prosecution's case was clear-cut, and it was presented crisply. Platoon Sergeant Russell testified to the late-night discussion on September 4, when Duffy said he was going to have the prisoner shot. Then two members of Lanasa's firing squad testified to the actual slaying on September 5.

The prosecution's case was airtight. We couldn't dispute the facts. There was ample evidence of conspiracy and that the shooting took place. We couldn't take the government to task in those areas.

It came down to this: I had to challenge the Army's war policy. I had to try to demonstrate that in this war, by real or implied orders from above, front-line troops were required to produce high body counts. And that this policy encouraged soldiers to dispose of Viet Cong captured in the field. I would try to show that the Army should shoulder the blame for what Duffy did.

My defense followed these lines: Duffy is a clean-cut, all-American boy. He joins the Army and becomes an officer. He's fervently patriotic and anxious to be a good soldier. He's trained to follow orders and that's exactly what he does. In ordering Do Van Man executed, he believes that he is acting according to accepted behavior and that superiors encourage and approve such behavior.

But Duffy is no murderer. Sure, he made an error, a grave error, but by no means an uncommon one. It was one hell of a dirty war and many good kids were dehumanized into thinking that blowing away Viet Cong prisoners was advancing the cause.

The problem of course was that what may have been accepted practice in the steamy jungles was a felony in a court of law. Execution of prisoners was illegal—a war crime.

So, shaky or not, our best hope was to take the Army to task over its body-count philosophy. This would offer us at least a fighting chance of saving Duffy's neck. Whether or not the jury accepted our argument entirely was a minor part of the gamble. Our main objective would be to present the jury with a legal escape route, a moral, logical reason for them to avoid reaching a guilty verdict. Also, to get an acquittal, it would be necessary to call a parade of character witnesses to the stand. The body-count policy was to be our pivot and character evidence the positive thrust.

Following this strategy, we called a string of Duffy's fellow officers to testify: all stated that it was battalion policy not to take prisoners because they weren't wanted.

First Lieutenant Ralph C. Krueger said, "My policy was that a man does not surrender during a fire fight. If a VC comes out of a fight to give himself up, that man is dead."

First Lieutenant John Kruger, a young West Pointer, then told the court, "Our policy was that once a contact was made we kept on firing until everything in the kill zone was dead."

Then came a bombshell. During his cross-examination, the prosecutor asked Kruger, "Have you ever killed a prisoner?"

"Sir," came the reply, "I can't answer that."

"Why not, lieutenant?" asked Judge Wondolowski.

"Sir, I'm afraid that if I do I could subject myself and people under my command to proceedings under the Uniform Code of Military Justice," Kruger said.

There was a stunned silence. Here was a brother officer, a comrade of Duffy's, invoking his Fifth Amendment rights on the very issue that was responsible for Duffy's indictment. Kruger was laying himself on the line when he could so easily have skirted the issue and denied any wrongdoing. His testimony could be the cornerstone of Duffy's defense.

To reinforce our case, we brought in two psychiatrists as expert witnesses. Dr. Stanley L. Portnow said that Duffy "believed he was doing the right thing." The other doctor, Wilbur A. Hamman, testified that Duffy "did intend to kill but with justification because if he turned the prisoner loose or sent him to battalion headquarters, the Viet Cong suspect would more than likely be released and return to the field to fight Americans."

But just when it seemed our defense was making excellent progress under tough conditions, the prosecution threw a monkey wrench into the proceedings. The prosecutors, Captains Herman Bate and Robert Bogan, filed a motion requesting that Judge Wondolowski throw out the body-count issue because it was invalid and hadn't been sufficiently supported by defense testimony.

If this motion succeeded, Duffy's defense was ruined. You can't defend a man charged with murder on character evidence alone.

One peculiarity of the Uniform Code of Military Justice that I have not mentioned before is that defendants found guilty of premeditated murder *must* be sentenced to life imprisonment. However, the sentence can be reduced on appeal.

Later that same day, Wondolowski announced his decision. "The motion is granted," he said. "Mr. Rothblatt, you will refrain from any reference to body count and factors relating to body count."

This was it, then. Very little more could be done to help Duffy.

Two days later, the summations were completed, Judge Wondolowski charged the jury and they retired to consider their verdict.

It's always rough on the nerves when a jury is out. But in the Duffy case, it was like waiting for the guillotine to drop. Finally, the word came. "The court's in."

Back in the courtroom, Judge Wondolowski was already at the bench, a cardboard cup of coffee at his elbow and a half-smoked cigar in the ashtray. The courtroom was packed with correspondents who sat with notebooks and pens poised. The wire service reporters had already arranged to relate the verdict to the States speedily by using military phones. *The New York Times* detached a reporter from Tokyo to cover the case, which the paper had featured on its front page every day for a week.

"The court will come to order," Judge Wondolowski declared at length. "Mr. President, members of the court, have you reached a verdict?"

"Yes, we have, your honor," the president, Colonel Robert W. Shelton, replied.

"Lieutenant Duffy, you will rise and face the court," the judge stated, and Duffy rose and paced the few steps until he stood, ramrod straight, in front of Colonel Shelton. He saluted.

"Lieutenant James Brian Duffy. This court, upon closed session and upon secret written ballot," Colonel Shelton intoned, "have considered the charges of conspiracy to commit premeditated murder and on premeditated murder. We have found you guilty."

A chill swept the makeshift courtroom. Total silence followed.

And then a strange thing happened. Colonel Wondolowski announced, almost casually, that the verdict carried an automatic sentence of life imprisonment. The officers in the jury jerked upright in their seats. They shot questioning glances at one another. At length, Colonel Shelton blurted out, "No member of the court was aware that a life sentence was mandatory." Meanwhile, he and his fellow jury members looked as though they would rather be charging an enemy stronghold.

For the first time, Colonel Wondolowski seemed at a loss. But, as I would have expected from this innovative officer, it took him only a moment to come up with a satisfactory solution. "Would you gentlemen wish to reconsider your verdict?" he asked. The eight jurors breathed a simultaneous sigh of relief.

A short time later, the jury came back with a sharply reduced verdict. Instead of premeditated murder and a conspiracy to commit premeditated murder, they brought in findings of involuntary manslaughter and conspiracy to commit involuntary manslaughter. Rather than life imprisonment, Duffy's sentence was six months' imprisonment and a $1,500 fine.

Duffy, his military lawyers, and I were beside ourselves with joy and relief. One sour note remained. From the jury box, Colonel Shelton had announced openly that "The court deliberated very long on the ramifications to the Army of this offense." There it was in a nutshell. "Ramifications to the *Army*." Not to the accused, of course not. It was not justice that was the goal but a neat refurbishing of the Army's image—the brass's image of the Army.

Since the court had rejected my body-count defense in the Duffy case I was not going to be stubborn about it when Lanasa came up for trial. Anyway, I knew that I had a strong temporary-insanity defense and confidently expected to have Lanasa committed for treatment—which is how it worked out. I understand that Lanasa eventually snapped out of the abnormal state he was in.

His was a classic case. If you have been face to face with death or mutilation long enough, you will crack. If your superiors are so shaken themselves that they cannot recognize the state you're in, sooner or later you will seek death for yourself to escape the endless nightmare, or you will strike out at anyone you can conceive of as the "enemy." In your distorted view, a harmless farmer, his wife, and their child are all plotting to blow your testicles off.

The very fact that Lanasa had acquired an outstanding reputation for rushing in when all reason recommended caution was an indication to me that he was looking for death—his own as well as the enemy's.

Incredibly, the Army sent Lanasa out again on combat patrol while he was awaiting trial for the Do Van Man murder. He was injured once again, but I believe the Army felt some hesitation about awarding him still another medal, in view of the circumstances.

On January 9, 1974, there was a short article on *The New York Times* "Op-Ed" page that puts into words many of the feelings and reactions I experienced in Vietnam. It was written by an ex-soldier, Peter P. Mahoney. While I don't agree completely with all that Mahoney writes, I feel strongly enough about it to reprint it here.

When the United States Court of Military Appeals recently upheld the conviction of William L. Calley, Jr. for the murder of at least 22 Vietnamese civilians at My Lai, my old bitterness and disgust were stirred.

My background was very similar to his. I was a drifter of sorts before I enlisted in the Army in April, 1968. I was looking to find myself, or whatever it is that an eighteen-year-old looks for when he leaves home for the first time.

Soon after I joined, the Army offered to send me to Officer Candidate School because the loss of so many junior officers in Vietnam had forced it to lower the standards of admission. I accepted because it was the most challenging thing the Army had to offer me, and I figured that if nothing else the Army could teach me to be a man. I graduated as a second lieutenant at the ripe old age of 19.

The Army has a rather peculiar way of teaching prospective officers the qualities of leadership. If a person can tolerate being treated as the lowest form of life on earth, being subjected to incredibly sophomoric and often sadistic forms of discipline, and being told that nothing he does could ever possibly be correct, then somehow after six months this qualifies him to lead men into battle.

The reason for all this, they say, is to teach men to think under pressure. But this method doesn't teach how to think, it teaches how to obey—blindly and unquestioningly. In addition, many candidates get the mistaken impression that this is how to run their own platoons, which accounted for, I think, so many lieutenants in Vietnam dying from gunshot wounds in their backs, or grenades under their bunks.

We had to try to reconcile this obedience with another crucial lesson. Everything in Officer Candidate School is against the rules, so a candidate soon learns that rules must be broken for things to get done—a handy tip for the future in Vietnam. The only rule that was always followed was this:

Don't get caught. It was a big game; senior officers would obligingly look the other way if we showed "ingenuity," but if we were too blatant we would be "caught." Lieutenant Calley got caught.

The court rejected his appeal that he was only following orders when dozens of villagers were shot in March, 1968. I cannot defend him for what he did, but I can understand the circumstances under which it happened. I never participated in any so-called atrocity while I was in Vietnam but that was only a coincidence of time and circumstance. I could have—I had been trained for it.

The only guide that confused young men like Lieutenant Calley and me had in Vietnam was morality, and the Army had done its best to eliminate such a defective idea. If you do not disobey an unlawful order, you get into trouble, but all orders are considered lawful unless you can prove otherwise, usually at your own court martial. Nobody seems to have pointed out that the Army probably would have been more willing to try Lieutenant Calley for *not* killing those people.

Lieutenant Calley was foolish, but so were we all. How can we isolate and punish instances of criminality in a war that was totally criminal? Where is the logic of sending one man to jail for killing civilians with bullets and making heroes of others for killing civilians with bombs? Of course, that is the way of our society. Those who give the orders are never punished; only those who get caught obeying them are allowed to be crucified.

Mahoney was there. He felt the opposing pressures, the smell of death. He understood the dilemma of the soldier trained to obey without question, then held responsible for this obedience. It's hard not to be affected by his honest, sensitive words.

SEVEN

Cast of Characters
The Judge

SOME JUDGES will be surprised to read this, but I have what amounts to awe for the Bench. The judge who is fair in all things—his conduct of the trial; his attitude toward the defendant, the lawyers, the witnesses; his charge to the jury; and, should it come to that, his sentence—this judge is to me a noble work of God.

Most criminal court judges try to be fair. Some, however, have a strong personal revulsion against certain types of crime. The experienced trial lawyer knows exactly which kind of case to steer away from which judge.

One judge I know, who does not become unduly upset about a child molester, gets choleric at the thought of a burglar entering a house at night while the occupants are asleep. "You might have given these innocent people a heart attack," he exclaims as he hands out the maximum sentence.

Another judge reacts so violently to the presence of a loan shark in his courtroom that you can't help suspecting that he had some unfortunate personal contacts with these gentlemen.

From the defense lawyer's point of view, these judges have one saving grace. During a trial involving one of their hangups, they are so eager for a conviction that they commit error after error and the defendant gets a new trial after appeal to a higher court.

Some judges, sad to say, should not under any circumstances be sitting on the bench. That great jurist, Harold Medina, once said with justice that it must be a terrible ordeal

75

for a man who is not intellectually up to it to serve as judge and have to hand down legal opinions in matters beyond his comprehension. I know what Judge Medina meant, but in my experience it is often the most incompetent judge who is the most self-satisfied.

I remember one judge who flunked the bar exam eight times running. Shortly after he miraculously passed (I was not alone in suspecting skullduggery) he was appointed to the bench. His subsequent rulings indicated clearly why he had flunked so many times. But he was shrewd enough to acquire an able law clerk to cover for him.

Under our system of selecting judges, we get more than a few incompetents as well as a fair sampling of men without an iota of judicial temperament. I think of the surly chap who threw a heavy book at the head of a lawyer who had the temerity to question one of his rulings. Luckily, the lawyer ducked in time. The book thrower glowered like an angry ape while everyone in the room sat frozen in embarrassment.

How do such misfits get on the bench? Sometimes they have excellent political contacts. Being related to a leading politician doesn't hurt. A rich father-in-law who can make a generous contribution to a political party's coffers also comes in handy.

Because of such unqualified judges, justice frequently takes a terrible beating. During a trial, a prejudiced judge may seriously violate a defendant's rights. I recall one so-called jurist who would come to court day after day and, without turning a hair, reverse nearly all the rulings he had made the day before. His law clerk, going over the record, had spotted the errors and tipped off the boss that he had committed a few bloopers.

At a criminal law seminar in New York, Judge Nathan Sobel, of the Brooklyn Supreme Court made a very interesting, if frightening, comment. He said that the Supreme Court can hand down all the great, resounding opinions it wishes, but there will always be lower-court judges who decide that they don't like the rulings and calmly ignore them. For the most part, they do this in cases where they are confident there will be no appeal because of lack of skill or money.

Such judges also frequently ignore rulings of other appellate courts as well. I will never forget the frustration I felt as a young lawyer when I handed in an incontrovertible brief in a divorce case, only to have the judge decide against my client, apparently because he didn't like his looks, or mine.

When I tried to point out that the law was 100 percent in my favor, the judge said, "Go ahead and appeal." As he suspected, my client did not have the money to appeal, so he got away with it. One of the nice things about attaining some success and stature in the profession is that these arrogant gentlemen finally realize they have to watch their step with you.

Whenever I get depressed thinking about judges like these, I am comforted by the thought of the late New York Supreme Court Judge George Carney. Learned in the law, deeply humane, courteous to the lowliest of defendants, George Carney gladdens the heart of every lawyer who loves his profession. Would we had a hundred of him. Five former members of my staff have joined the courts. Each one is a model judge. Perhaps I have trained my staff well.

The conscientious judge carries a heavy burden. I will never forget the plight of one sensitive, deeply religious jurist. He had accepted a plea of guilty from a defendant on a grand larceny charge. The following week, the defendant came in with a new lawyer and asked permission to change the plea to not guilty and to go to trial. He said that he was innocent of the crime and had been misled into taking the guilty plea.

Permission to change a plea is at the discretion of the judge, and it is usually granted. On this occasion, the judge had become irritated by the delaying tactics of the previous lawyer and suspected that this was another ruse to stall the proceedings. Despite impassioned pleas, he refused.

That night the defendant hanged himself in his cell. The judge was never the same afterwards. Almost every time I saw him he would bring up the painful subject again. He seemed to be begging for reassurance that his action had been innocent and justified. But sometimes a deeply troubled mind cannot be comforted. When the judge died a few years later, I felt he did so almost with relief.

This profoundly sensitive judge was one of many such I

have known. I have seen him and others like him pacing their chambers hours on end as they balance the needs of society against the rights of a defendant. The thanks they get is often an ignorant blast from some tinhorn politician trying to impress the voters with his dedication to "law and order." It takes real courage for a judge to stand up for a defendant's rights in the face of public clamor about "permissiveness."

Some judges seem to have an uncanny instinct for the proper sentence. Until they pronounce it, the just-right disposition of a case is hard to imagine. However, the moment they spell out the reasons behind their decisions, the logic and justice of their thinking becomes crystal clear. This is no mean gift.

Ironically, some judges who were highly regarded as liberal, all-around great guys when they were lawyers, turn out to be miserable on the bench, treating defendants as dirt. Conversely, some lawyers scorned as backroom politicians become gracious, scholarly jurists. As they used to say on New York's Lower East Side: "Go know."

Judges have one problem that they wish would go away. One judge said to me recently, "Every time I walk down the corridor I know I'm being bought and sold." What he meant of course was that some courthouse con man was pointing him out to a defendant as a judge he "had in his pocket."

Some of these unethical types—who may know the judge slightly—will seek occasions to stop him for a moment's chat in sight of the defendant. Others enter the judge's chambers on some pretext. In either case, the con man reports that "everything is under control." Of course, he expects the scared defendant to pay him handsomely for "fixing" the case.

A common variation is the confidence man's getting a tip that a case is about to be thrown out completely on its merits. He then rushes to the defendant and tells him the great news. For a large sum he can guarantee to get the case dismissed. The frightened defendant has been spending sleepless nights agonizing. So he and his family rush about, begging, borrowing and stealing the required amount.

More than one judge has been given a bad reputation by the gossip of these liars.

JUDGES I HAVE KNOWN

Three That I Hate

There's the judge who has no use for *any* defendant. Sadly, he is clever enough to know how to railroad your client if you don't watch him carefully.

There's the former prosecutor who still has great rapport with all prosecutors, something like the feeling an ex-player has for athletes. To him, the D.A. can do no wrong. And the defendant's lawyer is a bum, little better if at all than his client. This type of judge is usually not an intellectual giant, and your job is to bring him up short with a sharply worded brief, or with oral references to high-court decisions. You have to convince him that he is flirting with a humiliating rebuke from an appellate court.

There's the judge who slyly gives you everything you ask, so he can't be reversed. But if your man is convicted, you have had it. He rubs his hands happily and throws the book at your client.

The Bargaining Judge

The judge told an eighteen-year-old defendant charged with burglary that he could not assign a Legal Aid Lawyer to him because he had money in the bank. Actually, the money was in settlement of an automobile accident claim, and was being held in trust for him until he reached twenty-one.

The young man came to me and told me the story, ending up by asking me to be his lawyer. I took him back and said to the judge, "If I'm going to represent this boy you will have to sign an order releasing $1,500 of the money he has in his trust fund."

"Henry," the judge said, "will you take a thousand?"
We settled on $1,200.

The Understanding Judge

It's all in the way you look at it. Most people are shocked and revolted by a person who exposes himself in public. I didn't know the judge before whom my client was brought and feared that he might have a thing about "sex fiends" and throw the book at him.

But the first words out of his mouth dispelled my fears. "What have we got here," he asked, "A dickey waver?"

It sounded innocent; vaguely patriotic, in fact. We arranged for psychiatric care and a sick but salvageable person got a break.

The Practical-Joker Judge

This fun-loving fellow would call an inexperienced young lawyer up to the Bench. "Counselor," he'd say to the unsuspecting lawyer, "Let me give you a tip. When you go back to your client, say to me that the defendant is living with his wife, that he's working, and that he's supporting his children."

The elated beginner would follow the advice and then His Honor would let him have it with both barrels, "But Counselor, my probation report shows that this woman isn't his wife. He beat up his wife and deserted her two years ago. The only job this weirdo has is running policy tickets. All of them, including his illegitimate children, are on welfare. One year on Rikers Island."

The young lawyer had been initiated, and this strange judge would sit back with a satisfied smirk.

Chief Judge John J. Sirrica—Activist Judge

The presiding judge at the Watergate trial of my clients accused in the break-in, John Sirica, was a new experience for me. Most jurists are familiar with the shelf-full of books I have written—with F. Lee Bailey or by myself—and they tend to give me the benefit of the doubt on tricky legal points. But in Judge Sirica's court, I always had the feeling he was about to glare at me and call out, "Marshal, take him away."

Sirica kept interrupting my opening addresses to the jury, before my clients decided to plead guilty, with suggestions like "Why don't you tell the jury what your clients were doing in the Watergate at two-thirty in the morning?"; "Why don't you tell the jury who hired them?"; "Why don't you tell the jury who's been paying them?" A little more of this, I thought, and an appeal looks pretty good.

Judge Sirica liked to say that he ran his court as he thought best and that if a higher court overruled him that was its concern, not his. In this he differed markedly from most judges.

I recall that on the few occasions when the late, scholarly Judge Albert Cohn, father of Roy Cohn, was reversed by a higher court, he lapsed into week-long depressions. Meanwhile, his assistant tiptoed around with a hangdog look.

Even before the case began, I had some lively exchanges with Judge Sirica. But I did once manage to get a smile out of him. I was arguing for a change of venue because of the overwhelming publicity the case had received. "Where do you suggest the case be tried?" the judge asked. "Name a place where the people don't know all about it."

"San Juan, Puerto Rico," I responded. "There's a federal court there that could try the case, and since the people there can't vote in our national elections, they couldn't care less about the president and his people. Besides, the weather is excellent for lumbago."

The Judge looked at me sharply. I could tell he was wondering how I found out he was having a bit of pain. Eventually he grinned and said he'd think about it. His lumbago must have improved because he denied my motion.

EIGHT

My Lai

AFTER THE Green Beret and the Duffy–Lanasa cases, you would think that I had enough of the Vietnamese morass. But along came another case I couldn't resist—defending Colonel Oran K. Henderson, commanding officer of the 11th Infantry Brigade, against the charge that he was derelict in his duty by suppressing information of the My Lai massacre.

The advantage this case had over the others was that it was tried at Fort Meade, Maryland, in pleasant, comfortable surroundings, quite a switch from the conditions in Vietnam where merely staying alive in the brutal heat, under General Abrams's genial hospitality, was a feat in itself.

The My Lai incident would probably never have come to light if a former soldier had not written a letter to Chairman L. Mendel Rivers of the House Armed Services Committee. This sensitive, honest letter points up the dilemma and the tragedy of My Lai.

The letter makes clear that My Lai was a threat to the American forces. It was covered with mines and booby traps and it was a launching area for attacks on U.S. soldiers. And let's remember that it was difficult if not impossible to tell a Vietnamese national from a VC guerrilla, a harmless old man from a Communist sharpshooter. Children, women and octogenarians were all capable of squeezing a trigger and many did.

But then comes the moral dilemma. Does this give American troops the right to line up hundreds of My Lai men, women and children and slaughter them like cattle? The answer of course has to be no, even though it's not always an obvious answer in the heat of battle.

Read the letter written by Ron Ridenhour of Phoenix, Arizona, the former soldier. I'm reprinting most of it here because nothing I could say would dramatize so well the background against which the My Lai drama was played. You will recognize "Pinkville" as My Lai and "Lt. Kally" as Second Lieutenant William L. Calley. Here it is:

March 29, 1969

Gentlemen:

It was late in April, 1968 that I first heard of "Pinkville" and what allegedly happened there. I received that first report with some skepticism, but in the following months I was to hear similar stories from such a wide variety of people that it became impossible for me to disbelieve that something rather dark and bloody did indeed occur sometime in March, 1968 in a village called "Pinkville" in the Republic of Viet Nam. . . .

In late April, 1968 I was awaiting orders for a transfer to Company E., 51st Inf., when I happened to run into Pfc "Butch" Gruver, whom I had known in Hawaii. . . . During the course of our conversation he told me the first of many reports I was to hear of "Pinkville." . . .

One village area was particularly troublesome and seemed to be infested with booby traps and enemy soldiers. It was located about six miles northeast of Quang Nhai city at approximate coordinates B. S. 728795. It was a notorious area and the men of Task Force Barker had a special name for it: they called it "Pinkville." Its mission: destroy the trouble spot and all of its inhabitants.

When "Butch" told me this I didn't quite believe that what he was telling me was true, but he assured me that it was and went on to describe what had happened. The other two companies that made up the task force cordoned off the village so that Charlie Company would move through and destroy the structures and kill the inhabitants. Any villagers who ran from Charlie Company were stopped by the encircling companies. I asked Butch several times if all the people were killed. He said that he thought they were, men, women and children. He recalled seeing a small boy, about three or four years old, standing by the trail with a gunshot wound in one arm. The boy was clutching his wounded arm with his other hand, while blood trickled between his fingers. He was staring around himself in shock and disbelief at what he saw. "He just stood there with big eyes staring around like he didn't understand: he didn't believe what was happening. Then the captain's RTO (radio operator) put a burst of 16 (M–16 rifle) fire into him." It was so bad, Gruver said, that one of the men in his squad shot himself in the foot in order to be medivac-ed out of the area so that he would not have to participate in the slaughter. Although he had not seen it, Gruver had been told by people he considered trustworthy that one of the company's officers, 2nd Lieutenant Kally (this spelling may be incorrect) had rounded up several groups of villagers (each group consisting of a minimum of 20 persons of both sexes and all ages). According to the story, Kally then machine-gunned each group. Gruver estimated that the population of the village had been 300 to 400 people and that very few, if any, escaped. . . .

When I arrived at "Echo" Company, 51st Infantry (LRP) the first men I looked for were Pfc's Michael Terry and William Doherty. Both were veterans of "Charlie" Company, 1/20 and "Pinkville." Instead of contradicting "Butch" Gruver's story they corroborated it, adding some tasty tidbits of information of their own. Terry and Doherty had been in the same squad and their platoon was the third platoon of "C" Company to pass through the village. Most of the people they came to were already dead. Those that weren't were sought out and shot. The platoon left nothing alive, neither livestock nor people. Around noon the two soldiers' squad stopped to eat. "Billy and I started to get out our chow," Terry said, "but close to us was a bunch of Vietnamese in a heap, and some of them were moaning. Kally (2nd Lt. Kally) had been through before us and all of them had been shot, but many weren't dead. It was obvious that they weren't going to get any medical attention so Billy and I got up and went over to where they were. I guess we sort of finished them off." Terry went on to say that he and Doherty then returned to where their packs were and ate lunch. He estimated the size of the village to be 200 to 300 people. Doherty thought that the population of "Pinkville" had been 400 people.

If Terry, Doherty and Gruver could be believed, then not only had "Charlie" Company received orders to slaughter all the inhabitants of the village, but those orders had come from the commanding officer of Task Force Barker, or possibly even higher in the chain of command. Pfc Terry stated that when Captain Medina (Charlie Company's commanding officer) issued the order for the destruction of "Pinkville" he had been hesitant, as if it were something he didn't want to do but had to. Others I spoke to concurred with Terry on this.

It was June before I spoke to anyone who had something of significance to add to what I had already been told of the "Pinkville" incident. It was the end of June, 1968 when I ran into Sergeant Larry La Croix at the USO in Chu Lai. La Croix had been in 2nd Lt. Kally's platoon on the day Task Force Barker swept through "Pinkville." What he told me verified the stories of the others, but he also had something new to add. He had been a witness to Kally's gunning down of at least three separate groups of villagers. "It was terrible. They were slaughtering the villagers like so many sheep." Kally's men were dragging people out of bunkers and hootches and putting them together in a group. The people in the group were men, women and children of all ages. As soon as he felt that the group was big enough, Kally ordered an M–60 (machine-gun) set up and the people killed. La Croix said that he bore witness to this procedure at least three times. The three groups were of different sizes, one of about twenty people, one of about thirty people, and one of about forty people. When the first group was put together Kally ordered Pfc Torres to man the machine-gun and open fire on the villagers that had been grouped together. This Torres did, but before everyone in the group was down he ceased fire and refused to fire again. After ordering Torres to recommence firing several times, Lieutenant Kally took over the M–60 and finished shooting the remaining villagers in that first group himself. Sergeant La Croix told me that Kally didn't bother to order anyone to take the machine-gun when the other two groups of villagers were formed. He simply manned it himself and shot down all villagers in both groups.

This account of Sergeant La Croix's confirmed the rumors that Gruver, Terry and Doherty had previously told me about Lieutenant Kally. It also convinced me that there was a very substantial amount of truth to the stories that all of these men had told.

Exactly what did, in fact, occur in the village of Pinkville in March, 1968 I do not know for *certain*, but I am convinced that it was something very black indeed.

On July 15, 1970, following its seven-month investigation, the Armed Services Investigating Subcommittee of the Committee on Armed Services of the House of Representatives issued its report. The subcommittee found that a large number of unarmed Vietnamese were deliberately killed by an American task force. After some discussion of the military climate surrounding the event and the "cumulative effects of the horrors, fears and frustrations which the men of 'C' company had been forced to endure," the report concluded:

What obviously happened at My Lai was wrong. It was contrary to the Geneva Convention, The Rules of Engagement and the Military Assistance Command Vietnam Directives. In fact, it was so wrong and so foreign to the normal character and actions of our military forces as to immediately raise a question as to the legal sanity at the time of those men involved.

Those men who stand accused for their actions at My Lai have, in the minds of many, already been "convicted" in the eyes of many around the world. These two tragic consequences might have been avoided had the My Lai

MY LAI 87

incident been promptly and adequately investigated
and reported by the Army.

Where did all this leave my client, Colonel Henderson?
In a very difficult position, obviously, since he had been the
commander of the brigade and supposedly responsible for
the "prompt and adequate" investigation the subcommittee
found wanting.

What kind of man was Colonel Henderson? Perhaps this
will give you some idea. Almost as soon as I entered the case, I
had the testimony and affidavits of four lieutenant generals,
seven major generals, three brigadier generals, seven colonels, seven lieutenant colonels, two majors and a captain—all
vouching for the integrity and honor of Colonel Henderson.
I'm confident that if I'd wanted I could have got half the
officers in the United States Army to speak up for Henderson.

In his utter decency, he reminded me of that other remarkable soldier, Colonel Rheault of the Green Berets. In some
strange way, the fact that I helped get the charges against
Rheault dismissed made me confident that we could do the
same for Henderson. About such men there is an unmistakable aura of honor.

While Colonel Henderson had a lot going for him, he was
the right man in the wrong place. Born in Indianapolis, he
went into the Army at twenty-three. He fought and was
wounded in three wars, and was entitled to wear four Purple
Hearts, five Silver Stars, five Bronze Stars, and the Legion of
Merit. These were not "You decorate me and I'll decorate
you" medals, the kind that Army people smile about. Henderson was the kind of man the Army has a special word for:
outstanding.

However, in the entire Army there was probably no officer
less qualified to conduct a grueling investigation of his men's
alleged misconduct. It was not in his nature to suspect soldiers'
motives, to ask probing questions, to back people into a corner
and break them down. He once said to me, "All my life I've
fought to get combat assignments. I don't like staff work. I
always like to get with the troops."

Henderson thought of combat soldiers as very special human beings, men with courage and ideals, men who were risking their lives in a miserable war. They were not pawns on a chessboard. To Henderson, all soldiers were his brothers. I was convinced that if a grenade landed close to him and his men, he would be the first to throw himself on it to save the others. He completely lacked swagger and "military presence." If you stood him alongside a Patton, you would probably never realize he was there.

The Henderson case had all the elements necessary for a flagrant miscarriage of justice. The Army's prestige had sunk to a new low after My Lai and the top brass was acutely unhappy. The situation begged for a scapegoat and Henderson, by personality and as the commander of the brigade involved, was a logical candidate for the role. Although Henderson refused to believe it, I strongly suspected that the West Pointers at the top of the Army heap were pleased that it was not one of their own who was being crucified. (Henderson was National Guard.)

After a few sessions with Henderson, I began to worry. Not about the charges. I could cope with them. But time after time, I would catch a brooding expression on his face. It reminded me of a character in Arthur Koestler's novel *Darkness at Noon*—the dedicated Communist who agrees to confess to political crimes he did not commit in order to serve the Party's interests. More than once I guessed, from the agonized look in his face, that he too was wrestling with this question. Could he best serve the Army by offering himself up publicly as a whipping boy? My answer to this was a resounding no. So whenever I saw that brooding look I quickly involved him in a flurry of defense activities.

Presiding over the trial before a jury of two generals and five colonels was my old acquaintance, Colonel Wondolowski. I realized that if the jury should find Henderson guilty our chances on appeal—always so good when you have an incompetent judge—would be nil.

The case against Henderson sounded impressive but like most cases built on public relations rather than solid fact, it was actually flimsy. It was based largely on the findings of the so-called Peers Report, named for Lieutenant General William R. Peers, who had conducted a full-scale inquiry. The version supplied to the court was so garbled and filled with errors that you wondered how so much time, money and energy could bring forth so shoddy a product. In the 406 pages alloted to Henderson, there were literally hundreds of errors including changes in transcribing tapes made when the Army investigators interviewed Henderson and other witnesses. There did not seem to be any skullduggery involved—just plain, dumb carelessness. It was hardly the kind of document that could convict a man of Henderson's stature.

As the trial proceeded the prosecution encountered further woes. Two helicopter pilots, Captains Hugh C. Thompson, Jr. and Jerry R. Culverhouse, had been touted as key witnesses against Henderson. Previously they said that they had complained to Henderson about the wanton killings at My Lai. On the stand, however, Thompson said the officer he had complained to was "sort of heavy set and balding." All eyes swiveled to Henderson, who was thin and brown-haired. It was truly a defense attorney's dream and a prosecutor's nightmare.

Thompson's machine gunner, Laurence M. Colburn, also a "key witness" was prepared to testify that he too had complained to Henderson, but it developed that early in the game the prosecutor had shown him pictures of Henderson and he had not been able to make an identification. After a few sessions with the prosecutors, however, Colburn's memory was miraculously restored. He was all set to put the finger on Henderson. If allowed of course, this could have provided grounds for reversible error. But Wondolowski realized that Colburn's testimony was hopelessly tainted and wouldn't even allow him to take the stand.

In justice to the machine gunner, I don't maintain that he was willfully lying. Memory long after the event is highly suspect. It should never be the basis for a conviction. Also, when an army noncom knows that his superiors have a certain view of a situation, it takes quite a lot of guts and stamina to hold to a different view.

The simple truth was that Henderson had indeed talked to

a number of officers and enlisted men in the field, even though he had taken over the brigade just one day before My Lai, and was given only two or three days to conduct his investigation. To a man, all the soldiers told him that about twenty civilians had been accidentally killed by artillery and helicopter gunship fire.

His belief that his men were telling him the truth was bolstered by a talk he had with Captain Ernest Medina, the company commander of the assaulting unit. Medina told him that he had killed a wounded woman because he thought she was about to throw a grenade at him. Outside of that incident, he maintained, there had been no deliberate killing.

Plain, honest officer that he was, Henderson never doubted his men. Perhaps, if he had been a professional investigator instead of a professional combat soldier, he might have suspected that they were lying. As it was, he felt convinced that his soldiers had behaved properly.

At the trial, however, Medina came forward with the truth. He had resigned from the Army, after being acquitted of murder charges based on My Lai. Now he told the jury that he had lied to Henderson about the civilian deaths. In fact, he knew that at least 106 men, women, and children had been killed, and he had lied about this to other army investigators as well.

The extent to which Henderson had been taken in by Captain Medina was indicated by Medina's own testimony: "Henderson asked me the approximate number of non-combatants killed. I gave him the number twenty, and that they were caused by artillery and helicopter gunship fire. . . . He said, 'Ernie, is there anything else I should know?' I told him there was not, that I was a father and had three children and I would not have allowed anything like that to happen." Medina succeeded beautifully in convincing Henderson that the charges of a massacre were a Viet Cong propaganda move.

Another witness who might have been helpful for the defense was unfortunately unavailable—Lieutenant Colonel Frank A. Barker, commander of the infantry task force. He had backed up Medina's original story that only about twenty civilians had been killed. Barker died in a helicopter crash a few months after My Lai, so no one could have known whether he too had been deceived by Medina or whether he had also deliberately misled Henderson.

During the trial, it quickly became evident that the Army had considered My Lai a successful operation and had openly described it as such to visitors. In fact, Henderson testified, after his initial investigation, the matter never came up again except in briefings for visitors.

As the trial dragged on, the Army prosecutors went into their Alamo-type defense: no hope, but fight to the bitter end. During this spell, Mary McGrory made some acute observations in her syndicated columns which I found accurate and amusing. Here is a sampling:

Col. Oran K. Henderson has been charged by the Army with failure to investigate vigorously what the specifications delicately call "reports of excessive killing of noncombatants" at My Lai.

If Henderson's chief counsel, Henry Rothblatt, has his way, however, it will be the man who more than a year later did investigate the massacre for the Army—Lt. Gen. William R. Peers—who will actually be on trial.

Rothblatt is obviously going to conduct a search-and-destroy mission against the top brass in the Pentagon. Early in the morning as the pre-trial hearing resumed, he was saying, "We in effect charge Gen. Peers with making false statements."

At the morning break he held a press conference in the courtroom and opened fire on Gen. William W. Westmoreland. If Col. Henderson had been derelict in his duty to report what went on at My Lai, then Gen. Westmoreland may have been "equally guilty of dereliction," said the aggressive attorney.

Rothblatt is a New Yorker, 54 years old. He has darting brown eyes, a long tongue, a pencil-thin mustache and a suspiciously luxuriant crop of wavy brown hair. He is obviously of the school that believes a trial is total warfare, and the Pentagon can expect heavy artillery, sniping, and no end of harass-and-interdict fire.

Rothblatt understands that a lawyer who cannot always offer good law can at least provide good theater.

No one seemed more entertained by Rothblatt's lively, armflinging interventions than the judge, Col. Peter S. Wondolowski, a man of heroic geniality, who sips coffee from a large brown mug shaped rather like himself.

After Rothblatt had pronounced himself "shocked"—a condition hard to credit to an attorney of his cynicism and experience—at some Army failing, and had heaped scorn on the earnest young prosecutor, the judge beamed on him.

"Thank you, Mr. Rothblatt," he said, as one might compliment a particularly good turn from a soloist.

Rothblatt knows that the Army is sensitive about its secrets, and he will demand every witness and every piece of paper that might reveal that Henderson, in his languid investigation of what Ronald Ridenhour called "something rather dark and bloody" that occurred at My Lai, was following a policy of suppressing events that could prove embarrassing to the Army.

As for the "suspiciously luxuriant crop of wavy brown hair," I take the Fifth. But Miss McGrory stated my opinion of the Peers Report accurately. If one of my law clerks put together something so shoddy, I would fire him.

But she was wrong in calling Henderson's investigation "languid." Henderson did everything he could to get at the truth about My Lai. He was thwarted by disloyal aides and by soldiers who feared that telling the truth would set them up as targets in a turkey shoot. Medina had actually warned one worried soldier not to talk about the incident and to be sure not to write to anyone about it, especially not to his congress-man.

Meanwhile, the prosecution witnesses were collapsing like tin soldiers. But I admired Major Carroll J. Tichenor's tenacity for the prosecution. He just wouldn't give up. He and Lieutenant Colonel Frank J. Dorsey, my associate in the defense, were tough and hard-hitting, but fair antagonists. In short, both represent the best type of military lawyer.

After almost four months of legal maneuvering and confusing, contradictory testimony by 106 witnesses—much of it proving the unreliability of human memory—the trial finally came to an end. The case was over but a basic question remained. Why My Lai? As Henderson said, it was going to take historians or psychologists to clear up that question.

The question of Henderson's innocence or guilt was a simpler problem for the jury. It took them less than four hours to decide. Major General Charles M. Mount, the court president, announced the verdict: not guilty.

Colonel Wondolowski congratulated defense counsel on its conduct of the case and had praise too for Major Tichenor. He told Tichenor, "The government won its case today, because any time there is a just and fair verdict, the people win."

Henderson had planned to retire after the trial, but his attachment to the Army proved too strong. He became the commander of the Reserve unit at Indian Gap, Indiana, the state of his birth.

People often ask me if it doesn't sicken me to have to deal with the depraved characters I defend. If I do sometimes have this feeling, it is more than balanced by the privilege of representing a man like Colonel Henderson.

NINE

Watergate and
My "Cuban" Clients

ONE FATEFUL night, a poorly paid security guard at the Watergate Complex in Washington noticed that someone had put a small piece of tape on the lock of a door to keep it open.

It was June 17, 1972, night of the break-in at Democratic National Headquarters. There has probably been more said on radio and television and more written in books and magazines about this episode and its awesome aftermath than about any other event in United States history.

I see no reason to repeat here what everyone already knows. (Although in questioning prospective jurors for the trial of my four "Cuban" defendants [actually only 3 were from Cuba] and James McCord, Jr., who were caught red handed, and E. Howard Hunt and G. Gordon Liddy, the puppet masters, Judge Sirica came across ten persons who had never read, seen or heard anything about Watergate!)

My excuse for reopening the subject here is that as lawyer for the men caught in the break-in I had a front-row seat at the early unfolding of that all-encompassing tragedy. From my peculiar vantage point, I was able to see and hear much that even today is not well known.

While we were presenting the "Cubans' " defense, I got a call one day from Les Whitten, columnist Jack Anderson's personable and brilliant associate. When, he wanted to know, were my clients going to plead guilty.

"Never, to my knowledge," I told him.

"Well," he said. "I know you're not lying to me, Henry, but you'd better check again because I just found out that they are."

Whitten of course was right. He had better contacts than I did, including somebody at the Justice Department.

I argued myself hoarse trying to get my clients to refuse a guilty plea and to continue with the trial—but to no avail. These men were a new experience for me. In any criminal case involving more than one defendant, there is usually a frantic race to obtain lenient treatment. Honor among thieves is a myth. But everyone in the Watergate group refused to turn on their manipulators. During an interview that I arranged with *The New York Times* to offset damaging leaks from the prosecutor's office, Bernard Barker, one of my four "Cuban" clients, said that they regarded themselves as steadfast soldiers, even though they had been made scapegoats.

Since I refused to go along with the guilty plea I had to get out of the case. It was a terribly frustrating experience but I didn't blame my clients for not being able to accept my reasoning. Even the federal prosecutor, a reasonably able man, could not understand why I was withdrawing from the case and openly mentioned his puzzlement to the press.

Bernard Barker told the Senate Watergate Committee during a public session, "Our lawyer, Mr. Rothblatt, didn't want us to plead guilty. He is a very good lawyer but what could we do? They found us in the place."

I felt strongly that there was a great deal they could do. For starters, we could put up a pretty good defense based on the lack of the essential element of any crime—criminal intent. These fiercely anti-communist, anti-Castro militants, long used to CIA and other government undercover operations, actually imagined that they were working on a national security project to thwart the nation's enemies!

Secondly, I had a hunch that the government would refuse to disclose certain "sensitive" evidence to which the defense was entitled. This would afford grounds for dismissal of the charges. Although at that time I shared the rest of the country's ignorance of the existence of the presidential tapes, I had a strong suspicion that there was dynamite lying around waiting for someone to plunge the detonator.

Finally, I was sure I could get at least a few jurors to sympathize with these defendants who were, after all, only pawns of more sophisticated plotters. This could lead to a mistrial followed by protracted bargaining and an eventual plea to a reduced charge and lighter sentences.

Although my clients didn't take my advice and fight to the finish, we have remained good friends. Now that they are out of prison, I see them from time to time in Miami. They all have the Latin machismo that may seem ridiculous to some. I confess that I find it somewhat attractive. These men seem to me to be a throwback to a simpler, perhaps more colorful age.

Anyone who practices law as long as I have develops a kind of animal instinct for danger. By the time the jury had been selected and I had made my opening address, I began to sense that unseen forces were at work. Perhaps something I happened to say struck too close to home. Soon my antennae began to pick up faint signals—a whisper here, a glance there. All this suggested to me that the Nixon administration was not going to allow a "Henry Rothblatt circus on Watergate."

Some Washington poobahs were still smarting over my "obstreperous language and conduct" in the Green Beret, My Lai, and Duffy cases. The knowledgeable Nicholas Von Hoffman had this to say in his column:

". . . the chances of this case ever going to the jury are getting smaller and smaller. Too many powerful people don't want those witnesses blabbing stuff in open court that might connect this demeaning little episode to a Haldeman or an Ehrlichman. Already with E. Howard Hunt's guilty plea, the mysterious Donald Segretti's name has been struck from the list of prosecution witnesses.

"And," Von Hoffman noted, "Henry Rothblatt, the attorney for the four Cuban Libres, seemed to be reduced to using main force to prevent them [from pleading guilty.]"

I am certain that, had I agreed to go along with the guilty plea for my Watergate clients, a sizeable stack of hundred-dollar bills would one day have appeared at my office door, and been ushered in with shrieks of joy by my associates. But, as one of my "Cuban" clients said to me in a moment of exasperation with my stubbornness, "You don't speak their language." He referred of course to the behind-the-scenes manipulators who controlled the exchequer.

As it turned out, my agreeing to a guilty plea would have made it appear likely that I had been paid off to make the coverup look more legitimate. There are a lot of near misses in the practice of law. As Army officers kept warning me in Vietnam, "You have to watch your ass every second."

The Watergate plotters succeeded in getting me out of the case, but I managed to help prevent them from covering up many of their sins. My four "Cubans," as well as James W. McCord, Jr.—a client in a related civil case—released me from my responsibility to protect privileged conversations I had had with them. I was therefore free to appear as a witness before the prosecutor to tell what I knew. It's heartening to reflect that I played a small part in helping to uncover the plotters' campaign irregularities, their criminal misconduct in Ellsberg's psychiatrist's office burglary, their wholesale illegal wiretapping, their arrogant misuse of government agencies—including the IRS—to harass their enemies, their unlawful corporate contributions, their handy shredding machines, and all the other incredibly amateurish chicanery.

Attorney General Richard Kleindienst expressed a picturesque if overly tolerant description of how the perpetrators of these inanities felt when they were exposed. "They were embarrassed, like a thirteen-year-old boy caught masturbating," he said. To me, it seemed more like rape.

After he was arrested and deep in trouble, E. Howard Hunt said to me one day in his lawyer's office: "You know, when I was with the Company [CIA], you were trained that when things go wrong, you keep your head and prepare for emergencies. But those s.o.b.s in the White House had never had that training. They lost their heads."

More than a year after I got out of the Watergate case, a high White House official told a friend: "Maybe it was a mistake to get Rothblatt out of the case. If he stayed in, he might have used up his energy fighting with Sirica instead of with us." He had a point there. One of Judge Sirica's favorite sayings was, "You can argue until Doomsday. That is my decision."

In a *New York Times* story, Seymour M. Hersh wrote that I was "known to be angry over the reported outside pressure on his clients . . .'' That was the understatement of the year. I was furious, even though I understood their loyalty to their hero, Hunt. After all, Barker said that he would follow Hunt "to hell and back." Barker and the three others copied Hunt's guilty plea.

During the trial, I wished for the first time that I could be the prosecutor, with a couple of my own investigators from New York to help me. I would have kept the courts busy for years with indictments of the bribers, corruptors, and conspirators. Most of what I knew then became public knowledge, little by little, in the long months that followed.

There was a secrecy risk in having this "hot" information so early. I am a gregarious individual, and the same drive that sends me around the world impels me to orate freely on most occasions. Fortunately, I like beer rather than the more potent beverages that tend to loosen the tongue. In any event, I did not drop any bombshells—although I can sympathize with the unlucky young lawyer for Common Cause who played a subpoenaed White House tape for friends at a party.

I was not the only one who didn't like the way things were going in court. After Hunt and then my clients pleaded guilty, and Liddy and McCord were convicted, Judge Sirica made it known that he was unhappy with the way the case had been handled. "I was not satisfied during the trial," he said, "and I'm still not satisfied that all the pertinent facts that might be available have been brought out."

I agreed. That was precisely why I was fighting so hard to stay on the case. I believed that I could bring out those pertinent facts one way or another. In open court, the press would be there to report the truth rather than the usual lies the manipulators knew so well how to present convincingly.

After his conviction, McCord did finally begin to talk. What he told Judge Sirica in general terms about political pressure to force the defendants to plead guilty, about perjury during the trial, and about higher-ups being involved in Watergate caused a sensation. Even so, it lacked the direct impact and lasting effect that testimony in open court—with names, dates and places—would have had.

One innocent victim of Watergate is much in my thoughts as

I write—Martha Mitchell. I had come to know her four years before Watergate when she sought my advice on a legal matter. In some ways, she resembled the flighty Southern belle of fiction, but she also possessed a good deal of courage and common sense. John Mitchell recognized these qualities in her and would have done well to take her into his confidence before he got into deep waters. She never approved of Mitchell's leaving his lucrative and satisfying law practice to follow his chief into the Watergate morass.

During Mitchell's early troubles, Martha was a source of comfort and support. She continued to struggle as the tide of revelations involving her husband intensified. When the full extent of the catastrophe became apparent, her world crumbled around her. Her frantic telephone calls to the press made her a figure of fun. People had no way to discern the agony and humiliation that were at the bottom of her outbursts.

Perhaps I was prejudiced in her favor because I was aware of her basic decency and her loathing for the arrogant actions of Nixon and his coterie. In Martha's mind, there were certain things that gentlemen just don't do.

Inadvertently, I once put Martha in an uncomfortable position. I was representing McCord in a civil suit against the Committee to Reelect the President. Our claim was that the committee had hoodwinked him into taking part in Watergate by assuring him that they had the President's O.K. I needed Martha's testimony at a pretrial examination. Graciously, she agreed to come to my New York office. She was followed by the usual army of newspaper and TV people. Once again she was made to appear an amusing eccentric. I wish that those who delighted in ridiculing her could have seen her in my office, answering difficult questions about her husband and his associates with clarity and composure.

As the White House kept "explaining" Watergate and other capers, I remembered the phrase that my good friend, the late assistant district attorney Andy McCarthy was fond of using: "If you told that to a jackass, he'd kick your brains out." And the Democratic donkey did, indeed, kick a lot of Republican "brains" out before it was all over.

At least one person was pleased with the outcome of the

case. Attorney General Richard Kleindienst told a news conference, "I am satisfied both from the standpoint of the U.S. Attorney and the Federal Bureau of Investigation that they did an outstanding job." But another government official was not quite so complacent. "It makes you wonder," he said, "when top-level White House guys go around leaving false names."

It was not just this gentleman who wondered. With good reason, the whole world wondered.

TEN

Cast of Characters
The District Attorney

IT PAYS for the criminal lawyer to get to know the D.A.s, the men and women who will be his constant antagonists. And let's remember that many judges were once district attorneys themselves.

Most district attorneys are ethical and hard working; some are brilliant. But I have met very few who meant it when they told a jury, usually with a catch in the voice, "Why, I'd sooner resign my position than be a party to convicting an innocent man."

The truth is that district attorneys are ambitious, self-interested human beings like you and me. Most are eager to win victories in court to prove that they are worthy of being selected for the bench. So we can't expect them to be delighted when they lose a case, even a weak one.

It takes an unusual combination of qualities to be a good prosecutor. He must be aggressive and uncompromising when necessary, but he must also be able to recognize the difference between a vicious criminal and a victim of circumstances.

A lot of D.A.s don't understand their role. As prosecutors they are quasi-judicial officers. Their job is not to gain convictions—and newspaper headlines—but to see that justice is done. It is their duty to present all the evidence and to try a case fairly and to indulge in no foul play. It's as much their duty to clear the innocent as to convict the guilty. All this and more is spelled out in the *Code of Professional Responsibility*, published in 1971 by the American Bar Association Project on Standards for Criminal Justice.

Moreover, the prosecutor may not suppress evidence favorable to the defense, or even make a judgment as to whether any evidence might be valuable to the defense. This principle of due process and fair play is so important that an appeals court will order a new trial even when the prosecution suppresses evidence through negligence rather than through wilful misconduct.

This aspect of the prosecutor's job has been affirmed by the courts. For example, the United States Court of Appeals (in *United States* vs. *Zborowski*, 1964) granted the defendant a new trial, ruling:

> The prosecutor must be vigilant to see to it that full disclosure is made at trial of whatever may be in his possession which bears in any material degree on the charge for which the defendant is being tried. In the long run it is more important that the government disclose the truth so that justice can be done than that some advantage might accrue to the prosecution toward ensuring a conviction.

Now, this is the law. Yet many a prosecutor has used testimony which he knows or at least suspects to be untruthful. And many a prosecutor has made improper value judgments on specific evidence. Actions of this kind, whether or not they constitute deliberate obstruction of justice, taint justice badly. But every criminal lawyer of any experience knows that such things go on.

Some D.A.s do understand their jobs. Burton Roberts was such a D.A. I recall a case involving him. I had come into the case late—after the defendant was convicted. I was able to show that the policemen lied in their testimony and moved for a new trial. Roberts consented to set aside the verdict and dismissed the charges.

In large cities, the D.A. doesn't prosecute many cases personally. The New York County D.A. has a staff of 250. Even so, the D.A. will occasionally try an important case, especially if he feels the need of a bit of publicity.

Two men in former New York District Attorney Frank

Hogan's Homicide Bureau—now judges of the New York State Supreme Court—have impressed me as being close to model prosecutors. One, Burton Roberts was a formidable opponent, who has never allowed himself to become dehumanized. Another, Edwin Torres, is of the same mold. When you went up against either you knew you had better be prepared, because they would test every link of your defense. If there was a weak link they were sure to find it. And their own cases were solidly built.

Hogan's office was the best I have ever known. Thomas Dewey, his predecessor, started the tradition of efficiency and honesty, and if anything, Hogan improved on it. It's said that before Dewey anyone with $10,000 could buy a murder-charge dismissal provided the case was not too hot—a cop killing or some other sensational front-page homicide.

There was one D.A. I know was sincere when he said that he would rather resign than convict an innocent man. Andy McCarthy, of the Bronx, was a deeply devout and decent man. Although he could get angry at a hardened criminal, Andy was a world apart from another district attorney I knew who acted as if every defendant he prosecuted was the worst fiend that ever lived. Summing up to the jury, this man's face would turn crimson as he shrieked his hatred and fury. He got convictions by overpowering weaker personalities. Nobody was surprised when he died of a stroke at an early age.

There is one district attorney who hates the sight of me because years ago I was guilty in his eyes of a terrible breach of propriety.

I was representing a middle-aged defendant in a statutory rape case—one involving sexual intercourse with a willing female under the age of eighteen. The young lady in question was only sixteen, but she had been around and had a flair for earthy language rare in one so young. She had written the defendant a few letters, remarkable for their candor and colorful expression. Among other intimate details, she assured him that he was "the only one I let do this to me except those two fellows in Brooklyn, that sailor I told you about, and my regular boyfriend from Connecticut."

What exasperated the district attorney to the edge of apo-

plexy was that I proceeded to read the letters in their entirety
to the jury, unprintable words and all. This of course was not a
legal defense. It doesn't matter what the morals of the under-
age female are so long as the jury is convinced that the defendant had intercourse with her.

This jury took the easy way out, as so many juries do in
similar situations. They simply pretended to believe that the
act had not taken place.

The district attorney was infuriated—especially in view of
the acquittal—because I had read such vile language out loud.
I am sorry not to share his delicacy—which I had not previously noted—but fortunately I do not depend on his good
opinion for my peace of mind.

When a hot-headed district attorney continually loses ver-
dicts to a particular lawyer, it soothes him to believe that his
opponent is unscrupulous, unethical or a purveyor of per-
jured testimony. This can lead the enraged D.A. to try to "get"
the lawyer who has been making him look bad. Indeed, one of
the occupational hazards of criminal practice is the threat of
indictment. Even Clarence Darrow and Judge Samuel Leibowitz were indicted. And my friend and colleague, F. Lee
Bailey, was indicted because of a business association.

There was no reason to worry about Lee Bailey. The Florida
federal prosecutor who got him indicted had as much chance
as a house cat with a Bengal tiger. Still, I was unhappy about
Lee's involvement with business deals when he should be
concentrating on the law, a field in which he is a rare genius.
Unfortunately, Lee constantly craves action, and when the law
fails to provide enough excitement, he strikes out in a dozen
directions. If Consolidated Edison could harness his energy
there would never be another New York blackout.

A district attorney does not have to work very hard to get a
lawyer indicted. Once his intent becomes known, there are
always plenty of unsavory characters around eager to ingra-
tiate themselves with tales describing how the lawyer offered
them bribes, and tried to get them to commit perjury and
otherwise break the law.

Most criminal lawyers are alert to the danger and try never to interview witnesses without the presence of a third party, usually an office associate. This I suppose is comparable to the caution of a doctor who will not examine a woman patient unless a nurse is present.

Occasionally, even a fair-minded district attorney may step out of line in the heat of a court battle. But there's no excuse for a summation like this one in *People* vs. *Mull*, an early New York murder case:

Now I have made considerable and extensive inquiry, carefully, at a considerable expense, from a great number of your neighbors concerning each one of you that sits there. You probably observed that I had a little history here of each one of you. I know a good deal more about you than you think I do concerning . . . every man who sits in these chairs. I could not let any other person sit. It has been reported to me that you are very decent, square, upright, honest men. And if there is a man that sits in those chairs that is willing to brand himself with suspicion by saying that Archie Mull did not commit this crime, my judgment of his character is not at all correct. . . . It is no wonder that your neighbors have concluded that the integrity and decency of this panel of jurors, instead of Archie Mull, is on trial here today. Don't let it be said, don't let it be said, I beseech you, that twelve honest men cannot be found within the borders of Rensselaer County; don't let it be said of you that, from all the integrity and virtue and respectability of this great country, twelve men cannot be gotten together who will do justice. A failure to convict in this case, where there is no defense and where there is no doubt, cannot fail to create again another epidemic of murder in this county. It cannot fail to bring within our borders hordes of desperadoes and criminals, who rely upon the puerile inefficiency and weakness of jurors here, and will select this as a safe field in which to operate. The consequences of your failure to convict in this case, in my judgment, cannot be weighed or gauged or measured at all. How could a more brutal, wanton and pathetic tragedy be committed than this? . . . .

Outrageous? Yes, but you can hear variations of this summation every day in courts throughout the country. Often, they are delivered by lazy or ineffectual prosecutors making a desperate last-ditch effort to force a guilty verdict down a jury's throat. The message is always the same: Convict or you betray your fellow citizens. Sad to say, some juries do not have the guts to resist this kind of moral blackmail.

Of course, the district attorney knows—or at least should know—that a higher court is going to reverse the conviction, as it did in the Mull case. However, the D.A. who is intoxicated with his own eloquence can't restrain himself. And the district attorney making a bid to the public for higher office is beyond caring. Whatever the reason or motive, such summations are shoddy stuff.

ELEVEN

Caught in a Weird Web

I'VE ALREADY mentioned the unfortunate tendency of our law enforcers to come down hard on minority and "disadvantaged" suspects. Ironically, there's also a tendency to believe the worst of millionaire defendants who live high and enjoy exotic lifestyles.

Consider the weird case of young Mark, wealthy son of a manufacturing multimillionaire, father of three attractive children, with an attractive wife.

Young Mark had a self-destructive weakness for low company. Too late, he learned that you cannot roll in mud without getting dirty. He learned too that when a rich man ventures into the human jungle he becomes an irresistible morsel for the predators roaming there.

In 1964, Mark was charged with the first-degree murder of his bookie, Rubin (Ruby) Markowitz. The key witness against Mark was a prostitute with whom he had been intimate, Gloria Kendall.

F. Lee Bailey and I were retained very late in the case and didn't play any part in the actual murder trial. My career is too far along for me to strike a pose of modesty, so I will say right out that the verdict would have been different if we had been in on the proceedings from the start. Here's how the case developed, as Lee and I learned from the court records.

Gloria Kendall was an old whore in terms of experience, although not an unattractive one in her mid-thirtyish, big-breasted style. She had begun her extralegal career as a fourteen-year-old shoplifter in Rochester, New York, and five years later was doing her voluptuous best to satisfy the sexual lusts of the city's male citizenry. According to Rochester police

records, Gloria "Took a man to Claridge Hotel, had intercourse and while he was in the bathroom, took $125 from his
trousers and sneaked out. Admitted same."

The Rochester authorities frowned on Gloria's penchant
for such pranks and gave her two and a half years behind bars
to consider the error of her ways. To no avail. Upon her
release, she promptly resumed her previous lifestyle and
quickly drew another six months behind bars. Upon release a
second time, she decided that she was no longer welcome in
her hometown and took off for whoredom's Shangri-la, New
York City.

While Gloria had been to bed with countless men, she married only two of them. Understandably, both of them had
impressive criminal records. Michael Lazarus, husband
number two, was a particularly interesting specimen not only
on his own account but also because of his two "beloved"
uncles, hoodlums Lee and Richard Schlessinger. The latter
had an interesting speciality in light of the Markowitz murder:
he was given to sticking up bookmakers.

It was this speciality that drew the police to Richard Schlessinger when Ruby Markowitz was murdered. They got a court
order allowing them to tap Schlessinger's phone, stating that
they had been informed "by persons in a position to know . . .
that Richard Schlessinger and others were implicated in the
murder of Rubin Markowitz, whose body was found on
November 8, 1963 at Spuyten Duyvil Bridge. . . . Information has been received that Richard Schlessinger is engaged in
armed robberies of bookmakers. . . . He has seven previous
arrests for vagrancy, possession of counterfeit money and
various narcotic violations since 1951 and is a narcotics user
. . . investigation indicates that Schlessinger may be engaged
in unlawful activities. The motive in the slaying of Markowitz,
a bookmaker, is believed to have been robbery."

Gloria was very fond of her rascally uncle-in-law and she
managed to get him neatly off the hook in the Markowitz
killing. She told the district attorney a colorful, detailed story
accusing Mark of the murder.

In the pretrial publicity, Mark was branded a rich profligate, unfaithful to his wife and ungrateful to his hard-working, respectable father. It is not too difficult to imagine that the jury was predisposed to believe that such a man would kill his bookmaker to avoid paying the $7,200 lost on a baseball bet when Sandy Koufax humiliated the Yankees in the 1963 World Series.

Mark suffered another disadvantage because of his moneyed background. Around this time there had been a lot of heated comment on the unfairness of the judicial system to poor defendants who languished in jail while rich ones had little to fear from the law. Because of the intense media interest in Mark's case, no judge or district attorney was going to give this rich man's son the slightest break, thus laying himself open to the charge of favoring the privileged while running roughshod over the disadvantaged.

And so, incredibly, the trial began. A logical suspect, Richard Schlessinger, was out of the picture. Mark, on nothing but the word of a convicted thief and whore, was on trial for first-degree murder.

The scene of the crime as described by Gloria, was the two-and-a-half-room apartment on East 63rd Street in Manhattan that Mark had rented under an alias to serve partly as a home away from home for himself and partly for Gloria's creature comfort. It was to this apartment, Gloria said, that Mark had summoned her on October 10.

Q: (by the district attorney): Now what is the next thing that happened?

A: Mark sat across the room from me and I sat on the couch. He said to me, "What do you think is in that trunk, Gloria?"

Q: What did you say?

A: I said, "I have no idea."

Q: And what, if anything, did the defendant say?

A: He said, "It's the body of a dead man, my bookmaker, Ruby." He said, "I had to meet him this afternoon to pay him the money that we lost on the Series. . . . And I met him at four o'clock. And he came up here. And we were talking. And we had words. And I shot him." He said,

"Please, Gloria, help me." He said, "There's nobody else I can turn to. I can't call any of my friends; I can't call my family. You're the only one. Please help me."

So I said, "Well, what do you want me to do?" So he said, "Help me get the trunk out of here and get rid of it."

And I said, "Do you think anybody heard the shot?" And he said, "No, Gloria, I don't." He said, "It was over an hour ago, and I have been watching. I have been looking out the window, and I haven't seen anything."

And so I said, "Well, you must have been a very busy boy." I said, "How did you get the trunk?" And he told me that he bought the trunk in Spanish Harlem; that it was difficult to get a trunk that size because of the language barrier.

If Gloria sounds cool and collected, remember that she was not easily shaken. She continued with her story in sublime confidence. She said she had got hold of a couple of friends—neither precisely a pillar of society—to carry the trunk down to a rented station wagon and dump it into the Harlem River.

One of the friends was Geraldine Boxer, a husky, masculine woman who was "very fond of Gloria"; she also admired Gloria because she was "very bright, very learned." Geri, as everyone called her, confirmed the trunk-dumping story.

The other friend, David Broudy, also backed up Gloria's story to the hilt. Broudy was also a good friend of Gloria's first husband, her second husband, and the latter's uncles, Richard the Robber and Brother Lee Schlessinger.

Broudy's approach to life can be estimated from his cross-examination at the trial:

Q: You knew what business Gloria was in, did you?
A: Yes.
Q: You knew she was a prostitute, isn't that right?
A: Yes.
Q: You knew she was a madam who had other prostitutes working for her?

A: Yes.

Q: Did she introduce you to some of her girls?

A: Yes.

Q: Did you, to use a classic expression, enjoy the favors of these girls, mister?

A: Yes.

Q: Did you pay the girl for her favors or did you pay Gloria?

A: I didn't pay anybody.

Q: You were for free, is that it?

A: That's right.

Q: Now, you were there often with Gloria, weren't you?

A: Yes.

Q: You would do anything to help Gloria wouldn't you?

A: Yes.

Q: And would you do anything in the world to see that nothing happened to Gloria, is that right?

A: Yes.

Q: You would lie for Gloria, wouldn't you?

A: Yes.

Broudy gave other evidence of his lack of squeamishness over little things like dumping murder victims. After they had done the job, the three dined at a cozy little French restaurant, filling the time between courses, he said, with "joking and kidding."

Perhaps you wonder why Gloria and her pals took the stand and claimed credit for disposing of a corpse and other crimes. There's a simple answer. They had been given immunity from prosecution in return for their testimony against Mark.

An important witness for the defense was an investigator employed by the law firm of Mark's father. Gloria had called Mark and asked to meet with him. Mark refused and sent the investigator, William J. Whelan, in his stead, to find out what was on Gloria's mind.

During the trial, Gloria admitted that she had met with Whelan on February 11, and asked him for money; but he wouldn't agree to give her any. The blackmail nature of this demand—she threatened to tell Mark's wife and father about his other life—was established by Whelan's own testimony. He quoted her as saying, ". . . if it ever comes to a showdown, I am going to protect the ones that are dearest to me, not Mark." Presumably these dear ones would include her two former husbands and Uncle Richard.

Why more credence wasn't given to Whelan's testimony I can't venture to guess. But it is a matter of record that eight days after trying to blackmail Mark, Gloria went to the police with the story that Mark had killed Ruby Markowitz.

In his summation to the jury, the district attorney took pains to ensure that the jury would not forget about Mark's wealth of worldly goods. "Are you going to allow this defendant with his fancy background and his duplex," he exhorted the jury, "to get away with murder because he was cute enough to select a woman like this, with her sordid background, to help him out, so that later on his attorney could wash her dirty linen in public . . . ?"

Note the "duplex," obviously a symbol for the height of indulgence as well as the depths of depravity.

And the D.A. was careful to impress on the jurors that Mark, despite his upper-class background, chose to be part of Gloria's low-life milieu. "It was his selection," he assured the jury. "He sought her out. He went to bed with her. He paid for her favors and paid for the favors she offered his friends. She was good enough for him in the privacy of a bedroom. . . . It was a cute trick to argue that, how can you possibly believe an old whore like Gloria Kendall?"

There was a great deal more testified to and argued about during the trial, but when all was said and done, the jury deliberated at length and chose to believe Gloria and her friends and found Mark guilty of murder in the second degree.

It's hard to fault the jurors on their verdict. They could not deliberate on what they had not heard in court nor could they consider evidence alleged to exist but not presented. Here is some of the evidence they did not hear.

Dagmar Generazio, one of Gloria's call girls, told the cops that one day in October, Gloria called her to ask if she could get a car "to move a heavy box." She remembered clearly that she got the call between three and four in the afternoon. But Gloria told the police that Mark had called her at *six o'clock*. Gloria was hard-pressed to explain why she needed help moving "a heavy box" more than two hours before Mark's call. Faced with Dagmar in the D.A.'s office, Gloria began to switch stories with the speed of a weathervane in a hurricane. Dagmar was never called to testify.

Nor did either side call two other potentially important witnesses—a mother and daughter, Mrs. Vera McNair and Mrs. Yvonne Bennett, co-tenants with Mark in the 63rd Street building. They told the police that just before dark they heard shots coming from *outside* the building, and from the *opposite side* of the building from Mark's apartment. They also said that they had seen a trunk in the lobby of the building for at least two days in "late September or early October."

But the most conspicuous missing evidence was that of the defendant himself. Mark had not taken the stand because he believed he would be acquitted without bringing more pain and disgrace to his family by admitting publicly his associations with the dregs of humanity, as well as to his addiction to both gambling and extramarital sex.

Unfortunately, this was a case that fairly cried out for the defendant's testimony. The evidence against him was flimsy indeed, dependent on the story told by Gloria and her underworld friends. No one came forth to support their claims. No one saw them leave the East Side apartment carrying a heavy trunk. No one saw them put it into a rented station wagon (no record of the rental, either.) No one saw them dump it into the river. Despite all the publicity on the murder and trial, no one could be found to back up any part of their story. And no blood could be found at the spot where Gloria said the murder had been committed.

Still, in the absence of Mark's testimony, the jury had to be content with what it was given: the stories of a rogue's gallery of characters who were far from being above reproach.

Mark's decision not to take the stand damaged his case in still another way. It's true of course that a defendant has the constitutional right to remain silent rather than testify in his own behalf. But it's also true that failure to testify is often construed as an admission of guilt. The judge instructs the jury not to infer anything from the defendant's not taking the stand, but human nature being what it is, the jury finds it difficult to comply.

Another key element that never put in an appearance in the trial was the famous trunk which Gloria claimed held Markowitz's body. It disappeared forever. But Markowitz's body showed up, as reported by members of a radio motor patrol:

DATE: November 8, 1963
NAME: RUBIN MARKOWITZ
SEX: M
COLOR: W
AGE: 40
TIME: 7:00 A.M.
PLACE OF OCCURRENCE: Junction of Hudson and Harlem
    Rivers, 225 Street, New York Central Railroad Bridge.
NATURE OF ILLNESS OR INJURY: D.O.A.
COMMENTS: M, W, 5'10", 180 lbs, wearing gray pants, dark
    socks, black low shoes, black belt, black tie. Body badly
    decomposed. The legs of the body were tied with a
    clothesline rope. The legs were tied together at the ankles,
    knotted behind with a clothesline, which in turn was tied to
    pilings.

How a body that had supposedly been in a trunk thrown into the river was later found tied to pilings was a matter of some embarrassment to the police and the district attorney. They finally "deduced" that the body could not have been tied to the pilings; it must have got entangled in the pilings after getting out of the trunk, like a dead Houdini.

There were four bullets in the body, two in the head and two near the heart. An interesting sidelight: Frank Serpico, then an unknown but already highly independent detective, thought the murder had all the earmarks of a gangland killing.

Immediately after the trial, before sentence was imposed, Mark's family retained Louis Nizer, who made a motion to set aside the verdict. Included in Nizer's motion papers was an affidavit by Mark stating that he was "absolutely innocent," that he did not take the stand "on the advice of my former counsel that the prosecution had failed to make out a case and that no jury would believe its chief witness who was a confessed disreputable character." Then he added:

I never, directly or indirectly, had anything to do with the killing of Ruby Markowitz.

My involvement in this matter is due to two things. First, my association with Gloria Kendall and her ilk, an association of which I am deeply ashamed and for which my contrition is endless. The second involvement stems from the first—a plan to entrap me and to extort money from me plotted by Gloria Kendall, surely with the aid of others. It was Gloria Kendall who called me to the apartment at 63rd Street on October 10th, and not I who called her. I then had no knowledge whatsoever of the murder of Rubin Markowitz, whether planned or already accomplished. It was she who astonished me by asserting that Markowitz had been murdered. My shock at this startling news grew to panic when she threatened that because the trunk was in an apartment associated with me, I would be involved in the entire matter. All that she asked was that the trunk be removed from the apartment. Her threat caused me to act stupidly out of blind fear instead of instantly calling the police.

I never saw the dead body of Rubin Markowitz. In the light of evidence newly discovered by my present counsel, it is clear to me that there was nobody in the trunk and that this was told to me only to set me up later for a blackmail scheme; which was done. Gloria later made demands upon me for money. Some payments were made by me; others I resisted. I paid money to her because I had been placed in a position where I was easy prey for a hardened blackmailer, even though I had nothing whatsoever to do with a murder.

Mark also said that "Gloria and Ruby knew each other and I saw them together on a number of occasions." Ruby, he said, was a "nice man" with whom he had "never had any quarrel or difficulty," and that he had paid him in full the $7,200 he owed him, and other money owed by "several friends."

Nizer's motion was turned down as were his subsequent appeals to the Appellate Division and the Court of Appeals. In the latter tribunal, there was a strong dissenting vote by Judge Stanley L. Fuld.

Judge Fuld, who later became chief justice of the Court of Appeals, had some forceful things to say about the case, especially with regard to the almost forgotten Dagmar Generazio. He criticized the prosecution for the "conceded non-disclosure and concealment by the prosecution of evidence which, in my judgment, might well have persuaded the jurors to reach a different verdict." Judge Fuld continued:

> The record reveals that a Mrs. Dagmar Generazio had given the prosecution information which was at odds with the trial testimony of the People's key witness, Gloria Kendall, and that such information had not been disclosed to the jury or to the defense. Such information suggested—or, at least, so the jury could have found—that Gloria, rather than the defendant, was responsible for the murder and thus had a compelling motive to accuse him of the crime. Since the case against the defendant admittedly depended on the testimony of Gloria, there is heightened significance in the fact, likewise not revealed, that Gloria had actually been confronted with this information, as well as by Mrs. Generazio herself, in the District Attorney's office immediately before she recanted (for the second time) her story against the defendant. . . . The concept of fairness, of due process, imposes upon the prosecution a duty to apprise the defense of evidence favorable to the accused, particularly when such evidence contradicts the testimony given by the People's witness in open court. This duty persists even though the defense might, by dint of a little more effort, have independently uncovered the evidence in question and even though the

District Attorney regards it as lacking in probative force or worthless. The prosecution is not privileged "to decide for the court what is admissible or for the defense what is useful." . . . The argument that disclosure would not have changed the verdict "overlooks the variant functions to be performed by jury and reviewing tribunal." It is for jurors, not judges of an appellate court such as ours, to decide the issue of credibility, and we should be particularly observant of this principle in the case before us, where disclosure might well have impeached the one witness without whom there would admittedly have been no prosecution.

These powerful statements by Judge Fuld, whom I deeply respect, served to confirm the opinions I had formed about the case. I am certain that if Mark had taken the stand, he would not have been convicted. I am also convinced that it was not in his nature to kill, and that it was completely true to Gloria's nature to grab money from anyone who had it, just as she had taken the $125 from the pants of the man in the Claridge Hotel in Rochester. In New York, she had raised her sights considerably: a well-heeled bookmaker who customarily carried thousands of dollars around with him and a rich playboy represented a perfect double play, the dream of every thief's heart. First would come robbery, then blackmail. Murder, if necessary, was not off limits. And then no more need for those $25 and $50 tricks with every Tom, Dick and Harry.

Be that as it may, Mark went to jail and began serving his time. His family continued to do everything possible to have him released. Pleas to two New York governors for commutation of sentence were turned down.

Then, in 1975, the New York State Legislature passed a law making those convicted of second degree murder eligible for parole after serving ten years.

When Mark's family asked me to try to get him released on parole, I agreed to begin proceedings at once. Quite apart from my interest in trying to lessen what I considered a gross miscarriage of justice, I hoped to reward Mark's father for his unflagging faith in his son's innocence and never-ceasing efforts to free him from prison.

From the resistance of the parole authorities, you would have thought I was trying to spring John Dillinger. They pointed out that Markowitz's widow was strongly opposed to Mark's release, and that her "strong written opposition to your parole . . . offsets to a great extent the letters submitted on your behalf. . . . Her active, negative attitude coupled with other possible negative community attitude does not promote the possibility for your successful parole at this time."

The only unfavorable attitude in the community belonged to Mrs. Markowitz, which was understandable. It was patently false that there was other expressed opposition to Mark's return to society. His family and friends were anxious and eager to receive him. His father, in his seventies and still active, was looking forward to his son's return to the firm.

Moreover, Mark's behavior in prison had been exemplary. Correction officers who had daily contact with him were recommending his release on parole, the psychiatric reports were favorable, and Mark had already been approved for furlough and work release. There was no good reason under the sun—or under the law—for refusing to release him.

After two separate, unsuccessful jousts with the New York State Board of Parole, I felt much like Don Quixote. But I decided to tilt at the bureaucratic windmill one more time.

In a thirty-one-item petition, with many sub-clauses, I accused the board of operating "in vendetta fashion"; cited the irregularities in its performance in considering the two previous petitions; thundered that the Parole Board's concern with Markowitz's widow's "active, negative attitude" was a "staggering admission" that it was allowing itself to be used to represent the highly subjective attitude of just one person in the community; suggested that the board was afraid, because of the publicity given the case, that a decision to grant parole would loose a flood of "public attention and possible criticism"; speculated on whether the "substantial wealth" of Mark's family and their continued efforts to obtain his release had made the board "reluctant to grant petitioner parole for fear his release will be suspected of being the product of special or improper influence"; and concluded that the board was "incapable of evaluating the release of petitioner in an objective, neutral and detached and lawful manner."

This time, at long last, success.

Mark was free. After twelve long years in prison.

TWELVE

Cast of Characters
The Lawyer

LIKE DISTRICT attorneys, clients and judges, criminal lawyers are not always models of deportment. I will never forget my first disillusioning experience as a young lawyer. I was teamed with an older lawyer; he represented the defendant in a stickup case, while I represented an accomplice to the crime. While preparing the case for trial, I suddenly realized that the lawyer was handing his client a detailed, skillfully concocted story describing how he "just happened to be" in the bar where the robbery took place, how a fight started, how he defended himself, and so on. All of this was completely imaginary, but very convincing.

Now a veteran of countless court battles, I can say that such conduct is rare indeed. Most lawyers listen carefully to their client's story, ask searching questions, and then decide on the best possible defense—based on the facts and the law.

I recall one case in which both the district attorney and the defense lawyer tried a bit too hard to slant the facts—to the amusement of onlookers in the courtroom.

Detectives on the stand testified that they had chased two defendants over a fence. The defense lawyer sought to establish that the fence was so high that this was impossible. If true, it would follow that the detectives were lying about the fence and the rest of their testimony would be suspect.

Apparently, the lawyer conveyed his intention a bit too graphically to his photographer, for the resulting photo showed a fence that looked about twenty feet high. The district attorney saw at once what was going on, so he sent his own photographer around. That technician brought back a photo that made the fence look about one foot high.

Perhaps the defendant's photographer dug a hole alongside the fence and shot his photo from the bottom. Maybe the D.A.'s man took an airplane view. Whatever the techniques involved, the jury was thoroughly bewildered. The judge finally settled the issue by taking the jury to the scene where they could see the actual fence in person. It was exactly six feet high.

The misuse of a camera is relatively unusual in a criminal case, although it is common enough in negligence cases.

Sometimes, through ignorance, lack of concentration or momentary stupidity, a lawyer will pull a boner. Consider the case of the hood who was being tried for the cold-blooded slaying of a business rival. The State had an open-and-shut case and a quick verdict of murder in the first degree seemed inevitable. But for some unaccountable reason the jury came back with a verdict of murder in the second degree.

The defendant drew a sharp breath of relief—but too soon. His lawyer, braced for a first-degree verdict, automatically arose and recited the formula, "I move to set aside the verdict as contrary to law and against the weight of evidence."

"Granted," said the judge, at once.

The defendant tugged frantically at his lawyer's coat. The lawyer awoke suddenly to the situation, turned pale and spluttered, "Your honor, I wish to withdraw the motion. We do not want to set aside the verdict."

"Request denied!"

The jury's verdict could not have been set aside had it not been for the lawyer's motion. As it was, the defendant got a new trial, was found guilty, and landed in the electric chair.

One day I watched a promising young lawyer make a psychological error. He had picked a fine jury in what was obviously going to be a lengthy case. Then in the jury's presence, he asked the judge to put them in quarantine until the end of the trial so that they would not be influenced by outside reports and comments on the case. The black looks that he got from the jury were a sad portent of the verdict to come.

Of course, he should have made his request to the judge outside the hearing of the jurors, and at the same time, he should have made sure that the judge would not reveal to the jury that locking them up was the defense counsel's idea.

When I pull a small boner, I console myself by recalling the time my meticulous friend, Edward Bennett Williams, became red faced because of his staff. Williams was representing Lawrence O'Brien, in his capacity as chairman of the Democratic National Committee, in a civil suit against my "Cuban" Watergate clients based on the break-in.

Williams's deadline for filing a brief or, as they call them in that jurisdiction, "points and authorities," fell on a Friday. His office, no doubt busy with its weekend golf schedule, called me to ask if I would extend the due date until Monday. Full of fraternal feeling, I said okay. Came Monday, no points, no authorities. So I called the judge in the case and asked for an immediate hearing on a motion to dismiss.

At the hearing, one of Williams's associates told the judge that they were about to file an amended complaint and that this would render the points and authorities superfluous, or, as lawyers like to say, moot.

"Nothing doing," I said.

"Nothing doing," said the judge, as he dismissed the case. On its merits, I must add.

Moral: Always bone up on the rules of the court where you are trying a case, especially of course if you are not on your own turf. Otherwise, your carelessness can cost you dearly. And if you have a boss like the painstaking Edward Bennett Williams, he will be very angry.

There is one cocky little lawyer I will never forget. He had practically no experience in criminal law but he thought he could beat an airtight case of premeditated murder. Since this was a crime of passion by a first offender, the district attorney offered to let the defendant plead guilty to second degree murder, which meant that he could eventually gain his freedom. But the brash attorney, who should have leaped at the chance to take a plea, advised his client to stand trial.

The most pitiful aspect of the whole case to me was the

touching gratitude of the defendant. In the death house, he thanked his lawyer "for all you tried to do for me."

I too had to learn the hard way that you can be an expert in one area and a pushover in another. I was riding high after a series of victories when I got my comeuppance.

A client of mine had pleaded guilty to assault. I persuaded the judge to give him a suspended sentence. One of the conditions of the sentence was that he get a job. Since he was a seaman, he naturally got a job on a ship.

As it happened, he was a Cuban national. When his ship got back to port he was picked up by the U.S. Immigration and Naturalization Service for deportation. As an alien convicted of a crime, he was bound to remain in the U.S. By shipping out he had done the worst possible thing.

This danger had not occurred to me. At that time, my ignorance of the immigration laws was truly monumental. Luckily I was able to resolve the matter by going back before the judge and admitting the whole sad story. He and the assistant district attorney agreed to set the sentence aside and dismiss the case. Finally, the immigration authorities got off my client's back.

At that moment, I vowed that whenever I sensed that there was the slightest chance that anything outside of my specialty was involved in a case, I would do some extra studying.

It always helps to prepare a case carefully and to act promptly. In one recent, difficult murder case, the winning move came early in the game.

The case revolved around the question: Was my client temporarily insane at the time of the murder? I quickly retained the two top forensic psychiatrists in New York to examine my client long before the district attorney got around to it. These experts agreed that my client was temporarily insane at the time. This left the district attorney nowhere to go. No qualified psychiatrist he could get at that point could match the prestige of the ones I had retained for my client.

I am not implying that the two psychiatrists would have reached a different opinion if the district attorney had retained them. But since I retained them early, they were able to

spend the necessary time and take sufficient pains to arrive at
their conclusions. I did not feel that I had been unfair to the
district attorney by beating him to the punch. There was no
doubt in my mind that my client was mentally incompetent at
the time of the crime, and I would have suffered great anguish
if a State-retained psychiatrist had mistakenly declared him
competent.

For every dull-witted or inexperienced advocate, there is a
resourceful one who concocts tricky little maneuvers. One
lawyer I know was defending a habitual criminal when he
came up with a wild brainstorm.

As already mentioned, the fact that a defendant has a record cannot be made known to the jury unless he takes the
stand to testify. In one way, this provision is a big help to
habitual criminals. On the other hand, the jury is apt to con-
clude that the fellow has something to hide if he doesn't take
the stand. This in spite of the fact that the judge cautions the
jury not to draw such an inference.

The lawyer pondered this problem and for answer came up
with this little drama:

At the end of the prosecution's case, the defendant, carefully coached and rehearsed, started toward the witness chair.
Like a flash his lawyer ran after him shouting, "Sit down, I
don't want you to testify."

"I want to tell my story. They've got to know I'm being
framed," the actor-defendant cried above the roars of the
anguished district attorney.

The lawyer dragged his protesting client back to the defense table, having brilliantly put over the idea that the
defendant would have testified willingly except for his inter-
ference. Meanwhile, the jurors remained ignorant of the
defendant's record. An acquittal followed in due course.

This little act may seem to verge on the unethical, but in the
rough and tumble of the courts almost anything goes. One
funny little lawyer used to convulse New York's criminal
courts when he practiced there. He was all but unbeatable
because of his gifts for comedy. A master of pantomime, he
would have the courtroom screaming with laughter five

minutes after the jury was seated. The prosecutor would complain bitterly as he saw his case blown out the window. Eventually the jury's verdict would represent a round of applause for a masterful performance. Now and then, a district attorney would try to have the little barrister held in contempt of court, but to no avail. The fellow was a deadpan comedian; he never indicated by as much as a smile that he was trying to be funny.

Of the same show-business school was a tall, ruggedly handsome lawyer. When his client was in a tight spot during a trial, he would put his head down on the counsel's table, hide his head in his hands, and sob uncontrollably. I was never completely sure whether or not this was an act. There was no doubt in my mind that he was emotionally unstable. In any case, the spectacle of this vigorous-looking man overcome by grief had a powerful effect on the jury. After one trial, a juror told me that the lawyer must have been convinced of his client's innocence, even though the evidence was against him. Otherwise, why would the lawyer have broken down in court as he did?

Even with a good lawyer, an innocent defendant is occasionally convicted. Suspects of unsavory character are especially vulnerable to this injustice.

I remember one fellow in Brooklyn who had been a charter member of a den of thieves. His pals soured on him for various reasons, including a suspicion that he was a stool pigeon. For old times' sake, they gave him the benefit of the doubt and contented themselves with merely throwing him out of the mob.

Shortly afterwards, the man was picked up on suspicion of a murder in the Bronx. As it happened, he had been innocently playing pool at the time with his erstwhile associates. He sent urgent word of his predicament and asked them please to tell the D.A. the facts. Soon he learned the worst. The gang was delighted to see him in trouble, and as for providing him with an alibi, however truthful, forget it. The ill-starred hood begged and raged, to no avail. As far as I know, he may still be in prison.

Another victim of injustice, also a less than admirable type, sold magazines door to door. Smooth in appearance and glib of tongue, he liked to combine business with pleasure. After selling a subscription to a housewife (he always put business first), he would make advances and occasionally found a willing partner in dalliance. On the day in question, he had ventured upon such a lady, but unfortunately for him, her husband returned home unexpectedly at an awkward moment.

The errant wife had her wits about her and quickly shrieked rape. A hurried attempt to escape, a call to the police, and the salesman was as good as convicted.

It didn't help the salesman's case a bit that the district attorney could prove that the people who bought subscriptions from this gentleman, with or without sociability, never got the magazines. To the already hostile male jurors concerned about the safety of their womenfolk, this was adding insult to injury. The salesman spent the next three years in prison.

In the ordinary criminal case, the lawyer has to deal with complicated clients, cynical judges, and aggressive district attorneys. In murder cases, he will probably also have to deal with expert medical witnesses, from pathologists to psychiatrists. He can easily be overwhelmed and made to look foolish if he cannot speak and understand their language.

The lawyer's weapons in this unequal battle are time honored. Cross-examining an expert witness, the lawyer reads a passage from a medical book. The testifying doctor states that the passage is sheer nonsense. A moment later the doctor is told that he himself wrote the book.

To break down an expert's testimony, some lawyers use this trick. They ask him if he is familiar with the work of Doctor So and So, an outstanding figure in his field. The witness, properly set up by the cross-examiner (that is, exasperated and made to seem less than scholarly) will sometimes answer hastily, yes, of course he is. Then the lawyer will dramatically reveal that there is no such expert. The witness is branded a faker in the eyes of the jury.

I consider this dirty pool and do not indulge in it. Besides, it may boomerang. The jurors may resent gratuitous humiliation of an obviously qualified witness.

One fact stands out about today's criminal courts. Unless the lawyer knows a good deal about narcotics, poison, bullets, firearms, anatomy, and lots more, he might as well stay home.

The ability to speak effectively is also a requirement for the successful criminal lawyer. Unhappily, oratory is a neglected art in today's courtroom.

I can remember listening to Sam Leibowitz as he held jurors and onlookers alike spellbound for an hour of his summation in a first-degree murder case. He described in gruesome detail every step in an execution from the administering of the last rites to the disposal of the lifeless body.

Sam was a master at evoking sights, sounds and smells. It was a rare juror who was not moved to pity, even terror, by his recital.

I am not ashamed to admit that I do not try to suppress my emotions during a trial. If I feel like pulling out all the stops—and I often do—the people in the next courtroom and possibly in the one beyond that are usually fully aware of it.

Arguments to the court and jury, especially summations, are mysterious things. Sometimes a logical, well-reasoned, grammatically correct appeal will fall flat, while another that wanders from pillar to post—and even seems almost incoherent at times—makes a strong impression.

Just recently, I reread my summation to the military court in the Col. Oran Henderson My Lai case and was a little embarrassed by it. Some of the verbs don't match the subjects and the whole thing doesn't hang together too well. Yet, while I was delivering it, I sensed that it was having a powerful effect.

I think the reason for this is that a lawyer instinctively takes his cue from the response of the judge and jury as he is talking. If he feels that they are reacting favorably, he may skip a section of his prepared argument and emphasize the part that apparently is going over well.

It is impossible to judge an argument's effectiveness by

reading it in cold blood months after the trial. You must be in the actual courtroom, sense the atmosphere, and note the lawyer's manner and the expressions of those listening to him.

Personally, I would be willing to speak gibberish if it helped my client, and I would be unhappy if I delivered an oration worthy of Winston Churchill that was followed by a conviction.

When the great Clarence Darrow came to the Bronx in a murder case, I remember that the prosecutors could hardly hide their scorn of his lack of polish and his seeming disregard of the tricks of the trade. They were convinced that he owed his renown solely to the worldwide publicity generated by the Loeb–Leopold kidnapping-murder case.

But before the case was over, Darrow wove a magic spell about that courtroom. The D.A. himself would probably have voted for acquittal. Darrow had the priceless gift of being able to speak to men's souls. That is the true eloquence. If you have it, you need little else.

On another level, I recall a case in which the late Samuel J. Foley, the district attorney of Bronx County, and a very fine one, was summing up in a murder case involving four defendants. To my surprise, Foley practically ignored all the arguments of the lawyers for three of the defendants and concentrated on breaking down the arguments of the fourth lawyer, a young man recently admitted to the bar.

Eventually I caught on to what was happening. Foley realized that the jury had been moved by the young man's quiet sincerity and his unassuming manner. So Foley spent his time urging the jurors not to let themselves be swayed by such irrelevant factors. Later, one of the jurors told me that Foley had hit on the one argument that could have dissuaded them from allowing the young man's appealing personality to color their judgment in favor of his client.

Some trial lawyers sum up their cases to juries in a conversational tone, with a no-nonsense, "let's reason this thing out together like practical men" manner. This low-keyed style works for some because many jurors distrust the courtroom spellbinder, suspecting that he is trying to put something over on them. From time to time, I experiment with this technique, figuratively sitting in the jury's lap. But invariably, after the first five minutes, I see a couple of arms (my own) waving in front of me and hear my voice taking on its normal note of near hysteria. To each his own.

Many years ago I watched an intriguing lawyer trying a jury case. I forget his name but he was a law partner of Franklin D. Roosevelt. The trial was in New York City, but this highly sophisticated gentleman managed to turn the courtroom into a country general store and the jury into a bunch of farmers sitting around the cracker barrel warming their toes at the cast-iron stove.

I couldn't believe my ears when he began to talk about "a three-teated cow" he owned. He had obviously bought his clothes from some traveling stock company specializing in hayseed comedies. But I can't recall whether he actually snapped his suspenders.

What is it that makes us respond so eagerly to the simple past? Nostalgia, or just plain dislike of what we have become?

Later on, I ran into one of the lawyer's associates and I asked him about his partner's curious trial manner. He laughed. "He likes to make the jury feel superior to him," he said. "He prepares his grammatical errors carefully before every trial. The only case he ever lost was when he got absent-minded and was his own snooty self."

In recent years, there has been much talk about the crisis in criminal law. If there is a crisis, it is due at least in part to the shortage of experienced and conscientious criminal lawyers. Today, the majority of bright law graduates are snapped up by law firms representing big business. The bulk of the others also find lucrative careers in tax and commercial law. Criminal law gets the leftovers. I never stop congratulating myself that I have managed to attract extremely able young people to my office.

We must find a way to have excellent lawyers trying criminal cases. Take a small example. To protect a client under our system, a defense attorney must recognize errors made by a judge and he must also make the necessary objections and exceptions for the record. Otherwise, except in rare first-degree murder cases, the appellate court won't even consider the errors.

If most of our brightest lawyers continue to head for Wall Street and assorted corporate boardrooms, we will end up with inadequate criminal lawyers. We will have lawyers who let their clients down. We will have lawyers who fail to spot a judge's faulty ruling, thus losing a chance for appeal. I have seen judges who, in their charges, do everything short of ordering the jury to convict, while the defense attorney sits staring dumbly.

To remedy this situation, I would like to see a committee of lawyers set up similar to the "tissue committee" in hospitals that determines whether an operation was justified or competently performed. Composed of reputable lawyers, such a committee would review the record in criminal cases and decide whether the defendant had been properly represented. This might come too late to help a specific accused, but it might serve to suggest to the ineffectual defense attorney that he take his talents, such as they are, elsewhere.

As I have mentioned, there are some very bright young lawyers in my office. Thank God! Now and then one of them comes up with an idea that makes me feel my age.

When we were discussing possible defenses for my Watergate clients, one of the younger men threw this on the table: "The National Committee is supposed to represent all Democrats. Two of our four clients who broke into the Democratic National Committee Headquarters are registered Democrats and were therefore entitled to be on the premises. Why was it wrong for them to be there?"

I said to myself, This young fellow will go far—but I don't know in which direction.

We have frequent staff meetings. Often a strange thing happens. I will start out arguing one point of view, with the others opposed. After much talk, I find myself going over to their side while they start edging over towards mine. Things get very confusing. But it's much better this way than for a single man to try to think of all the angles himself.

There was a cartoon by Robert Day in the New Yorker many years ago that still amuses me. Three lawyers are surrounded by acres of legal volumes. One lawyer says plaintively to the others: "What burns me up is that the answer is right here somewhere, staring us in the face."

The cartoon was funny because of its underlying truth. Usually, the legal answer is there somewhere. Unfortunately none of us is a computer. It is so easy for us to overlook the one element that will save our case.

To close this section on my beloved chosen field on a light note, I once opposed Edward Bennett Williams in a case. Williams was pressing one of my witnesses, a young lawyer, rather hard, searching for some essential information.

"What's your secretary's name?" he asked.

The young lawyer gave the name.

"What's her address?"

"I don't know."

"What, you don't know your own secretary's address?"

Rothblatt: "Ed, he never took her home."

The judge enjoyed it and Ed smiled, too. Even lawyers have to laugh sometimes.

THIRTEEN

Of Rape and Macho Lib

THE SUBJECT of rape is very much on people's minds these days. And with good reason. While the rates of certain other violent crimes seem to be diminishing somewhat, the incidence of reported rape is rising sharply. Some of the rise is without doubt attributable to the women's movement, which has encouraged victims of rape to report the crime rather than suffer in silent shame.

In terms of numbers, rape is a social plague of almost epidemic proportions. Yet the federal government has only recently taken official note of the scope of this national disgrace. In early 1977, the government established a National Center for the Prevention and Control of Rape, under the auspices of the National Institutes of Health.

This organization's function is to launch much-needed research into the psychological makeup of rapists, the laws dealing with the crime, and—most important—the treatment of rape victims. It's fear of embarrassment and humiliation at the hands of the police and of the courts that makes women reluctant to report rape attacks.

In 1976, Nan Robertson wrote in *The New York Times:*

> The doctor walked into the crowded hospital emergency room, and shouted, "All right, where's the rape?"
> To gasps of surprise, some snickering and a few sympathetic glances, the victim, burning with embarrassment, followed the doctor into the examining room. "O.K., honey, jump up on the table and let's see what the big bad man did to you," he said.
> This true story of behavior toward a rape victim,

once common among hospital personnel, the police and the courts in New York, is becoming much rarer now.

"Our supreme achievement," according to Gladys Polikoff, the new commander of the Police Department sex crime analysis unit, "has been to change the ingrained attitudes of the authorities dealing with rape victims, from 'she was asking for it,' to 'compassion and tact.' "

This is not to say that the tough-guy approach to rape victims has disappeared across the country. Rape victims are still treated as the accused—a guilty participant in the crime—in many sections of the nation.

Finally in 1977, New York State dumped a horrendous law that required a woman rape victim to provide witnesses to her own violation! In more than a few parts of the country, women are still required to take lie detector tests before a law enforcement official will consider prosecuting the crime.

So progress, while laudable, is still impeded by the antiquated but persistent notion that—no matter how it happens—a woman is wrong to get involved in extramarital sex. And that if she does, it is at least partly her fault.

It would help if the judiciary—men for the most part—got over the idea that rape is purely and simply a sexual crime. For instance, in 1977, the California Court of Appeals overturned a lower court's guilty verdict in a rape case on a legal technicality. The victim was a hitchhiker. The court also managed to strike a blow for "macho lib."

In a unanimous decision, Judge Lynn D. Compton declared: "It may not speak well of the prevailing standard of morality in society, but women hitchhikers should anticipate sexual advances from men who pick them up . . . [any hitchhiking female] advertises that she has less concern for the consequences than the average female."

Quite apart from the legal niceties of the decision, the language of the opinion outraged not only women's organizations but also many state legislators who had been advocating legislature to encourage women to report cases of rape and to testify in court about the crime.

It's difficult to understand how anyone of common sense could chastise a waitress for leaving her car to be fixed and then hitching a ride to her destination. Was she really looking for sex? Or just for transportation—in that community where public transport is nonexistent?

But, haltingly, things improve. In Madison, Wisconsin, a Dane County judge was accused of making sexist remarks in the dispositional hearing of a case involving three teenage boys accused of raping a high school girl in the stairwell of the school. The judge, Archie Simonson, stated that the boys had only reacted normally, given their ages, to the sexually permissive atmosphere of that liberal university community.

Judge Simonson was soundly defeated by feminist candidate, Mrs. Moira Krueger, in the next election. The former judge, now back in private law practice, did himself no good at all with such unjudicial pronouncements as: "It used to cost money in Chicago to see women wearing clothing now seen in public." Apparently, the judge got to see the sights in Chicago.

I don't usually shy away from unpopular causes or clients. So I have defended my share of men accused of rape. As a human being, I am deeply concerned with the physical and psychic hurt done to rape victims. As a criminal lawyer, I am perforce concerned with representing rapists and, with more enthusiasm, men falsely accused of rape.

For example, I successfully defended a young man accused of rape by a determined young woman. To force him to marry her, she first tried threats. When her threats failed, she decided to carry them out one evening. After sexual relations with the man, she leaped out of bed, banged her head against a radiator, let go with some piercing screams, and then rushed into a neighbor's apartment with a trumped-up story of rape.

The police arrived, a doctor found semen in her vagina, and a young man guilty of nothing underwent the horrendous experience of being tried for rape.

Fortunately for him, his "victim" was not as persuasive on the witness stand as she had been that night with the police. And the jury readily recognized that my client was telling the truth. I was happy that I did not have to cross-examine her with any vigor.

I have observed defense lawyers in court impugn the morality or stability of a rape victim to the point where she loses her
credibility. And women jurors in particular have shown themselves to be skeptical of alleged rape victims who are excep-
tionally pretty or well dressed.

In one case, a defense attorney apparently dredged up an
1836 New York State Court of Appeals decision (*People* vs.
Abbott) which did indeed imply that "nice girls don't engage in
sexual intercourse." He had the temerity to ask the victim,
"Did you ever scream, 'God help me, I'm being raped?' Were
you immobilized? Were your legs broken?"

This outrageous questioning obviously struck some responsive chord in the jury because it couldn't reach a verdict,
despite the fact that the victim had been knifed in addition to
being raped. That defense attorney is today a judge.

Happily, defense attorneys who go too far in their attempts
to blacken a complainant's reputation often see their tactics
boomerang. Endless questioning about a victim's past sexual
history, for instance, may so alienate the jury that a guilty
verdict is almost assured.

I recall sitting in one trial in which the defense counsel
asked the complainant, "How are we even sure this is human
semen and not animal semen?"

The jury gasped and the attorney recovered sufficient sense
of courtroom decorum to blush at his inane question. I wasn't
around at the outcome of the case but I wouldn't have bet a
nickel on the accused's chances for acquittal.

Trying to humiliate the complainant in a rape case is definitely not my style. But in looking through my files, I find a
number of cases in which my sense of moral outrage was
provoked by lying complainants.

In one case, a woman caught by her husband in flagrante
delicto kept her presence of mind and persuaded her spouse
that she was the victim of rape rather than unbridled passion.
The husband, who was large in physique if not in intellect,
beat the woman's lover half to death before hauling him off to
police headquarters.

The trial proved my client innocent, however unwise in his
choice of bed partners. This time the outraged husband took

it out on his wife when they got home, and he in turn was hauled off to the police station. I never did find out the outcome of this little marital drama. But I am reasonably sure that my client stayed away from married women from then on.

Perhaps the most bizarre rape case in which I represented an innocent defendant was one involving a disturbed, homely young woman who was starved for affection. She concocted a tale of rape that named as her attacker a handsome youth whom she knew only from a distance and had never met. Her fantasies were so vivid and her condition so pathetic that the jury was almost ready to believe her story.

The one positive aspect of that distressing trial was her agreement to undergo psychiatric treatment. I hope she is now well.

While some judges and lawyers still perceive rape as a strictly sexual crime, we have come to recognize that it is a crime of violence and aggression, of hostility and degradation.

Dr. Dorothy J. Hicks, medical director of the Rape Treatment Center at Dade County's Jackson Memorial Hospital in Miami, Florida, has called rape "the ultimate invasion of privacy." Her center treats an average of sixty-five rape victims a month, ranging in age from two months to ninety-one years. While most are females, about four percent are males.

In addition to working with rape victims, Dr. Hicks keeps in close touch with the treatment program for convicted rapists at South Florida State Hospital. Her study of this program, along with her own findings, has convinced her that rape "is not a sex act. It is a violent crime that has nothing to do with sex except that sex organs are involved. Rape is an attempt to humiliate a victim who happens to be vulnerable and handy at the time."

She has learned some intriguing facts about rapists, including the following:

- A good many of them began their criminal careers as "peeping Toms," and then turned from this form of invasion of privacy to the worst form of all.

- A high proportion of these offenders grew up in homes that were female-dominated. Even more surprising perhaps, a sizeable number of them had themselves been sexually assaulted during childhood.
- Over half of these men were married, and most of the married men had children. Although these rapists tend to attack at least one woman per week, the rapists' own wives were the last to suspect them.
- To these offenders, rape is a strong compulsion. The men revealed that when they weren't actually out raping a woman they were fantasizing about it.
- Rapists also tended to increase the violence of their acts as time went by, since it really was the violence—not the sexual satisfaction—that they craved. Even more frightening, they began to take weapons with them as they continue to rape. The danger is that, sooner or later, the violence turns to murder. The "ultimate invasion of privacy" becomes an irrevocable act of violence.

These findings have a special interest to me. Quite often in my career—particularly during the early years when I was frequently a court-appointed legal defender for indigent clients—I have defended men who were guilty of rape. I was not too upset in those days when a client who was a two- or three-time offender was removed from the streets for a decent interval. I did my duty as a court-appointed lawyer but I could feel little sympathy for these men, psychopathic—which means sick—though they may have been.

In some cases, however, I have felt sympathy not only for the rape victim but for the rapist as well, because I believed that he was not legally responsible for his actions. This does not mean that he was not cognizant of the consequences of his acts, but that he was a disturbed personality who succumbed to a vicious anti-societal drive over which he had no control. His actions were not motivated by greed or a drive for personal advantage.

In my opinion, it did not serve society well to place a man like this in prison with vicious offenders, in a situation where a fearsome inner-power structure is often maintained by prisoners who rape other male inmates.

Toss him in prison and throw away the key, or try to restore him to mental health and a place in society—that was the issue in many cases when, from a strictly yea-or-nay legal point of view, I didn't have the slightest shred of doubt about my client's guilt.

If there seems to be some moral ambiguity here, it comes with the territory. A defense attorney has to judge each prospective client as both a fallible human being and a fellow citizen who has the right to a properly mounted legal defense.

For example, back in 1966, I received a call from a parent in Washington, D.C. He had been given my name by a local attorney who told him that he was too busy to take on the case. Too busy, hell. He just didn't want to defend a rapist and probably realized that the case would require too much time in preparation to remotely compensate him.

My first inclination was pretty much like his. But the parents—the mother also called begging me to take the case—were so convincing in their distress that I knew that I wasn't going to say no.

They had no idea their son was a pervert—their word for him—and he had never been in trouble before and everyone thought of him as "such a quiet young man." Well, there was obviously something more than quietude lurking inside their son, because he was now in deep, deep trouble.

Harry Morrow was a slightly built young man in his mid-twenties, plagued by deep feelings of inferiority and inadequacy. Yet, by some complex psychological mechanism, he convinced himself that any female he raped would want to see him again. This irrational marriage of uncertainty and vanity is not uncommon to rapists.

Harry was caught because he cruised in the neighborhood of a recent victim, expecting that she would literally greet him with open arms. Instead, he was spotted, his license was taken down and he was picked up the next day.

None of this is unique. But even without the benefit of Dr.

Hicks's findings, my associates and I began to realize that rapists like Harry are not the single-minded creatures that the media and society have made them out to be.

Like other rapists, Morrow had many explanations and rationales for his crimes. This was a typical one: "I recall feeling as though I had not done anything terribly wrong. There seems to be a world of difference between what I did and the kind of rapist who beats a woman and leaves her for dead—tears her fingernails off, does a sadistic job."

Morrow also sounded at times as though he felt he had done his victims a distinct favor, although he said he had a strong need to apologize afterwards.

"Generally speaking," he told me in a pre-trial interview, "I was a good sex partner and my relationship with girls when we were in bed were always under my control. I had more difficulty out of bed than in it, and my fantasies when masturbating were always of the girl being very passionate—out of her head with my making love to her."

The psychiatrists who examined Morrow found him suffering from "an impulse neurosis," a catchall diagnosis usually applied to fetishism, sadism, and exhibitionism. He told the doctors that after he found that he could not maintain any healthy relationship with a girl he liked ("It's like they finally found out what I really was"), he decided "to screw anything that I could." His failure in personal relationships was a symptom as well as an aggravation of his illness.

Typically enough, Morrow started out as a peeping Tom, went on to a few abortive attempts at rape, and then, after conquering his fright, graduated into a full-fledged rapist.

As it turned out, Morrow was very lucky—for a strange reason. About that time, there were some widely publicized rapes, all of them committed by brutes who beat their victims mercilessly. The fact that Morrow had not injured his victims and that he had not been armed with a lethal weapon worked in his favor. Moreover, the psychiatrists did not consider him violence-prone. And even his victims felt more contempt for him than rage. His slight stature—and, to be perfectly frank, his white skin—didn't hurt either. The upshot was that he pleaded guilty to a misdemeanor and got a light sentence to be followed by probation and parole.

Part of our agreement with the district attorney was that Morrow would be treated by a psychiatrist for a period of no less than two years. During that period, I kept in close touch with the doctor to check on Morrow's progress.

While studies show that there is as high as a 57 percent recidivism rate among convicted rapists, those enrolled in a program of psychotherapy—where they work to understand the drives behind their antisocial acts—almost always stay out of trouble following their parole.

No one can claim that these men are reclaimed as "normal human beings"—whatever that means—but at least they have gained an understanding and insight into their past violent behavior and have learned how to resist whatever dangerous urges remain.

True, Harry Morrow received a light sentence. So far, he not only has stayed out of trouble but he has also "got his act together." Enough so that he recently was married. Good luck, Harry.

FOURTEEN

Cast of Characters
The Jury

SOME defense lawyers think they can pick a jury likely to acquit. They have all kinds of theories about nationality, race, age, occupation, and appearance. Some even go so far as to hire research experts to construct profiles of the "ideal juror" for a specific case. I have harbored such ideas myself from time to time, but I had an experience as a young lawyer that shook my confidence in the process.

The case involved a young husband who had taken a shot at his father-in-law with a .38 caliber revolver. I was delighted to find among the selected jurors a charming young lady my own age.

The case went well and I anticipated a quick not-guilty verdict. But the jury stayed out for hours and hours. As you may have suspected, the young charmer was the one and only holdout for conviction. I guess I just wasn't her type. Since then I have been reasonably careful about getting "good" juries but I don't have any feeling of infallibility about it.

Of course, I am not suggesting that the defense attorney should refrain from asking questions aimed at turning up quirks or prejudices harmful to his client. It's vital to excuse any juror who for any reason cannot bring an open mind to the case. Obviously, a man who has recently been mugged may find it difficult to be impartial in a mugging case. Because this aspect of jury selection is important, F. Lee Bailey and I devoted twenty pages to the subject in our *Successful Techniques for Criminal Trials*.

Some lawyers accept every juror—except those clearly

unqualified—with an airy wave of the hand, suggesting supreme confidence in their client's innocence. Sometimes I wonder whether these casual-appearing lawyers don't get as good juries for their clients as the lawyers who agonize over a lengthy list of "desirable" characteristics.

What I try to do is select intelligent jurors who understand that a person can get into trouble without any criminal intent. For example, a defendant may be absolutely certain and will testify under oath that he told something to a friend the year before. The district attorney brings in irrefutable proof that he actually spoke to someone else entirely. With dismay, the defendant realizes that his memory has betrayed him. In the eyes of the jury he is an outright liar. A worldly, fair-minded juror will be aware of the tricks memory can play and will make allowances for them.

First-time jurors are often surprised when the judge instructs them not to convict the defendant unless they are convinced of his guilt *beyond a reasonable doubt*. This may seem to impose an unfair burden on the prosecution, but a little thought will show that this rule of law is absolutely essential.

The fact is that a defendant can look guilty and yet be completely innocent. Coincidence, which can be incredibly weird, has trapped many an innocent man. Mistaken identifications have convicted countless others. The woods are filled with police buffs eager to impress the authorities; publicity seekers, and assorted idiots who get pleasure from seeing other people in deep trouble. All are familiar figures in the criminal courts. The best protection against them is the reasonable-doubt rule.

Juries should remember that a defendant may have been careless, stupid, weak, or even hateful. No matter. The juror's job is to consider only his guilt or innocence of the specific crime charged.

Here is an example of the kind of case in which the reasonable-doubt rule might have made a significant difference. A lawyer I know had defended a man on a charge of receiving stolen goods. The jury found the man guilty and the lawyer got him a suspended sentence.

About a year later, the same man showed up in the lawyer's office and asked him to help get him his citizenship papers. The lawyer, with his mind on a dozen other matters, agreed and got the necessary form for the man to fill out. The form was completed in the lawyer's office and the lawyer mailed it to the U.S. Naturalization Service.

That night the lawyer went home, had his dinner, read for a while, and went to sleep as usual. Suddenly, in the middle of the night, he woke up in a cold sweat. His subconscious had brought a horrifying thought to the surface.

One of the questions asked on the form was whether the applicant had ever been convicted of a crime. And the client had written "no." The lawyer quickly grasped the implications. Here he was—a lawyer who knew all about his client's previous conviction—and he had helped fill out a form denying that conviction. Could there be a clearer case of subornation of perjury?

The lawyer's action had been without criminal intent at all. He had been careless or sleepy or inattentive. But who would believe it? Weren't lawyers supposed to be smart?

Maybe you are wondering what all the excitement is about. Wouldn't the jury take the lawyer's word for it if he were brought to trial? Perhaps, but consider this. Suppose the client decided to save his own skin by blaming it all on his lawyer. He could very well claim that the lawyer advised him to deny that he had a record.

Happily, the lawyer immediately had the application called back, and the matter never got to trial. If it had, the reasonable-doubt rule would at least have given him a fighting chance.

Ideally, a juror should give the same credence to a witness different from himself in color, religion, or economic status as he does to one similar to himself in these respects. But I learned long ago that when I have an Irishman, a Pole, a black, a Puerto Rican, a Jew, or a member of any other minority on the jury, it is a pretty good idea to have a character witness for my defendant who shares the same background as that juror.

In one case in which I represented a prison guard accused

of beating up a prisoner, I had a jury including a member from each of the groups just named. So I contrived to have five characters to match.

I think I know why jurors react this way to witnesses of their own kind. Perhaps subconsciously they want to know whether the defendant is an enemy of their people. When they see one of their own testifying for the defendant, they are reassured on that point.

Along with judges and lawyers, jurors must be constantly on guard against the public hysteria that may easily lead to the conviction of an innocent man.

Some years back, there were a number of sex murders of children in New York City. Because a young man on the Lower East Side, where the crimes occurred, was thought to resemble a suspect, a raging mob gathered quickly to put him to death. Fortunately, the police arrived in time to save this completely blameless youth.

What struck me most was that even after the mob realized they had the wrong man, some of them were still ready to kill him because of the resemblance! Their statements to TV reporters were absolutely staggering. One burly character was asked how he would have felt if he had killed the man and then learned that he was the wrong man. He shrugged his shoulders and said, "Just one of those things."

From time to time, one finds a juror on the panel with this type of mentality. Given his way, he would reverse the old legal maxim that it is better for a hundred guilty men to escape punishment than for one innocent man to be convicted. If he is forceful enough, he may get a few pliant jurors to go along with him.

Luckily for justice in our courts, a large majority of jurors take their responsibilities most seriously. They are conscientious, interested, and eager to find the truth. They make our system work. What would happen to justice in the courtroom without them?

At least one of my clients owes his freedom to an alert, clear-thinking juror.

My client was accused of stabbing and killing a man in a

Bronx barroom brawl. At the trial, two witnesses testified that they saw my client kill the victim. They even agreed that he had stabbed the victim through the abdomen and up into the chest. They were certain of it.

Next, the medical examiner described the cause of death—a deep chest wound.

My defense in the circumstances was not an overpowering one. There was a free-for-all in the bar, I maintained. In the confusion of bodies kicking, punching, and shoving each other, it was possible that anyone could have committed the crime. How then could the witnesses be sure beyond a reasonable doubt that my client was the guilty one?

In spite of my oratory I was somewhat surprised but pleased when the jury failed to reach a verdict. Curious, I sought out one of the jurors and asked him what in my defense had struck a responsive chord with the jury.

"Well, the defendant couldn't be guilty," was his surprising answer.

"Why not?"

"Because both the witnesses said that your client stabbed the victim with an upward thrust. But the doctor described a wound that could only be caused by a downward thrust. So the witnesses must be lying."

Sure enough, at the next trial, I followed up the juror's observation. I pressed the two witnesses on the direction of the stabbing movement. Upward, they insisted as confidently as ever.

Their confidence evaporated when the doctor took the stand. When I asked him whether the wound could have been inflicted by an upward thrust, he said no, the wound had to be inflicted by a downward thrust. The jury believed the doctor.

Score one for the jury system.

FIFTEEN

Xaviera

ONE SPRING day in 1971, a beautiful, green-eyed, blonde woman walked into my office, causing a few heads to turn. She looked not at all like one of my run-of-the-mill clients. Her name, Xaviera Hollander; her occupation, madam of the now famous brothel at 155 East 55th Street, New York City. And yes, she wanted to retain me to represent her.

All bright and breezy, she told me her problem. For the second time, she had been arrested—even though she was paying $18,000 a year for police protection. This, she felt, was dirty pool. She thought that she was being framed because she hadn't agreed to pay an increase in protection money.

She wanted to contest the charges, whatever they might be. It seemed to me that there was a fair chance to get the case thrown out, so I agreed to act for her.

She went on to tell me about herself. She spoke seven languages fluently, she said. Back in Europe, she had been voted The Netherlands' Most Outstanding Secretary. As unlikely as this sounded, I could believe it. In fact, listening to her, there was little I felt her incapable of.

She tired of her native country, Holland, and migrated to South Africa, where she met a young American business man. They became engaged. When he returned to the States, she duly followed, planning her wedding en route. But something happened and the engagement was called off.

Penniless, she was forced to find work. Fortunately, her seven languages came to the rescue. She got a job with the Dutch Diplomatic Mission to the United Nations.

But New York is an expensive town. Soon Xaviera was

"turning tricks" during her lunch hour, then in the evenings, and then all night long, until finally she was too tired to type and took to prostitution full time.

Being smart as well as good looking, she was soon running her own whorehouse, the classiest in New York City. Her clients included the wealthy and the successful—politicians, doctors, judges, corporation presidents, even lawyers.

The account books Xaviera kept were truly marvelous. Along each one of hundreds of names, there were one or two phone numbers and addresses (Xaviera was big on Christmas cards) along with notations about each client's personality, physical charactcristics, financial responsibility, sexual quirks, and so on.

Xaviera was even tolerant of her difficult customers, although she was put out if their checks bounced too often. Typical account book entries: "very sweet"; "lively person"; "very nice, sweet, young"; "very nice, was married to a hooker" (I forgot to ask Xaviera whether this fellow was entitled to a discount); "lovely advertising man"; "lawyer—talks a lot"; "groovy little guy, genius"; "smart"; "sweetheart."

One client earned the entry "pain in the neck." Another was described as "phony, never pays, snotty." One customer was identified as "gynecologist." Another was starkly described: "drinks vodka." One deadbeat had given Xaviera a phone number that turned out to belong to the Police Department. And a visitor from Canada was so enthusiastic about Xaviera's establishment that she noted that "he wants similar operation in Toronto."

Xaviera was never one to mince words. She complained once to columnist Earl Wilson that Mayor Lindsay and the police were "harassing us hookers."

"Why," she asked, "is Mayor Lindsay cracking down on call girls while taxis carry ads for massage parlors where every man knows he can get all the action he wants for five, ten, or twenty dollars?"

The articulate Xaviera was a persuasive debater. "We call girls provide a social service," she said. "The business should be legalized. We don't hassle anybody, we don't rob anybody. I have very intelligent girls and I run a respectable house. I don't see why they should harass us."

That Xaviera had grounds for feeling hassled was indicated by the proceedings of New York's Knapp Commission, which was investigating police corruption in the city. Here is part of a taped conversation between a policeman and a friend of Xaviera. A is the friend and P the policeman:

A: What are we talking about in figures—approximately?

P: So, if she wants to give like two or three hundred for the division.

A: Well, how's it work . . . division, borough and precinct?

P: And precinct, yeah.

A: Two hundred.

P: That's reasonable . . . Well, the precinct you can probably buy for two.

A: Two hundred?

P: I think . . . I think . . . you could wrap the whole thing up for between 800 and a thousand.

A: Yeah, look, you gotta have a little for yourself. We appreciate that.

P: Well, listen, she said I got a hundred dollars a month for myself, right?

A: Right.

P: The only thing that would happen is the chief, something like that, the P.C. (police commissioner)—I can't control that.

A: The chief of what?

P: The chief inspector.

A: Yeah.

P: And the police commissioner—I can't control them.

A: Who is it—you mean downtown?

P: Yeah. That's the heavies, that's the heavy. A lot of time they get a communication down there and pass it from the chief inspector to the borough—beautiful. But if they come up themselves then you're [obscenity]. But you got like ninety-eight percent guarantee, no matter how, ninety-eight.

A: That's eleven hundred a month?
P: Right.

On the morning of the trial, Xaviera told me, "Henry, don't worry. It's all fixed." She went on to say that the arresting officer was now a friend of hers and was going to play down the charges.

"Xaviera, policemen just don't change their stories like that."

"This one will because I've bribed him," she said.

I exploded on the spot. I couldn't imagine anyone as bright as Xaviera doing anything so dumb—and dangerous to her lawyer as well. "Xaviera, you might know a lot about men and all but let me tell you about the facts of life," I almost shouted. "You don't go behind your lawyer's back and bribe cops or witnesses."

To which she said, "Well, I thought you're so straight that you wouldn't do it."

I tried to explain the possible consequences of her bribing the cop but to no avail. Probably, her years of paying protection money had convinced her that that's how things are done.

There was still a little time before court opened so I rushed over to the D.A.'s office and asked him what he would give me—lawyer's talk for plea bargaining. The D.A. said that if she would plead guilty, he'd lower the charge to loitering, a misdemeanor.

So that's what happened. The judge generously fined Xaviera only $100.

As we left the courtroom, Xaviera kept complaining that it had cost her $3,000 to bribe the cop and he didn't even have to take the stand. The fact that she was let off with only a $100 fine didn't impress her. "Three thousand dollars for nothing," she kept repeating.

There was of course a very good reason for not going along with Xaviera's "fixing" the cop—besides the ethics involved. Had the cop admitted on the stand that the defendant had given him $3,000 to change his story, the assumption would most likely have been that I was a party to the deal. I could be tried for conspiring to pervert the course of justice, among other charges, all of them felonies. And how could I prove my innocence? There's practically no way in the world. Chances are I would have been nailed. And conviction for a felony means automatic disbarment. A sad epitaph for a successful criminal attorney.

Although Xaviera was not jailed, she was hardly in the clear. Her call-girl house figured prominently in the Knapp Commission investigation. She became a notorious figure overnight, throughout the United States and in Europe as well.

An undercover agent, Teddy Ratnoff, conned Xaviera so beautifully that he became her "financial advisor." He bugged her brothel and put her clients under surveillance. The resulting tapes were turned over to the Knapp investigators. Nothing was ever proved against the public officials and politicians among her clientele, but the general outraged hue and cry put Xaviera out of business.

But prostitution's loss became literature's gain. In collaboration with Robin Moore and Yvonne Dunleavy, she wrote her life story, appropriately called *The Happy Hooker*. It was a huge best seller, with over seven million copies sold.

All this notoriety nudged the Immigration and Naturalization Service into taking an interest in Xaviera. The I.N.S. soon discovered that she was an illegal alien, having violated the terms of her visa. Near the end of 1971 the I.N.S. instituted deportation proceedings against her.

Xaviera decided that she needed a "straight" lawyer and called my office. I represented her at the immigration hearing and managed to get a stay of the deportation order for a couple of months.

Eventually, Miss Xaviera Hollander departed these United States. She went to England and stayed there a while. She returned to North America and settled in Toronto, where she wrote a follow-up best seller to *The Happy Hooker*. Perhaps she is now busily perfecting her piano playing—another one of her talents.

Truly a remarkable, colorful woman. We will not soon see her like—at least not in New York.

SIXTEEN

But for the Grace of God

JOE SAVARESE, as I will call him, was a decent average young American caught up in a financial bind. With a little bit of luck, he might have steered clear of trouble. But economic stress, temptation, and a series of maddening circumstances combined to undo him. Slowly, inexorably, he allowed himself to drift into taking a serious misstep.

You would think that a bright young man like Joe Savarese would have begun to feel that he was stepping beyond the bounds of good sense and called a halt before he went too far. But his willpower was weak and the needs of his growing family strong. How many of us faced with his problems would also lack the moral strength to fight clear of the trap he fell into?

Let me give you part of his story as he told it on the witness stand:

Q: Mr. Savarese, are you the defendant in this proceeding?
A: I am.
Q: What is your occupation?
A: I am a chiropractor.
Q: State your educational training.
A: I am a graduate of the University of Pennsylvania, I received my bachelor's degree in June, 1956. I was a graduate of the Columbia Institute of Chiropractic, and I received my Doctor of Chiropractic in December of 1967.
Q: Mr. Savarese, you mentioned that you have the title Doctor of Chiropractic. Are you a medical doctor?
A: No, sir, I am a chiropractor.
Q: Following graduation in 1956, what did you do?

A: I entered the service, the U.S. Army, as a second lieutenant in May of 1957.

Q: When you entered the service, how long were you on active duty?

A: I was on active duty for six months until November, 1957.

Q: After that did you have a reserve obligation to meet?

A: Yes, sir. An eight-year obligation, and I was honorably discharged in 1965.

Q: Going back to 1956, did anything else happen in 1956?

A: Yes, sir. I was married in November of 1956.

Q: How long were you married to your first wife?

A: My first wife passed away in 1961, in September. I was married approximately five years.

Q: Do you have any children by your marriage to your first wife?

A: Yes, sir, one daughter, Maria. She'll be twelve in June of this year.

Q: Does Maria live in your present house?

A: Yes, sir.

Q: After you returned from the Army, what did you do?

A: My first position was a selling position with an anesthesia equipment company selling anesthesia equipment.

Q: What happened in August of '58? What did you do then?

A: I changed my position, and I got what was a better position and one that I had wanted more, as a pharmaceutical detail man with Charles Pfizer & Company.

Q: How long did you work for Charles Pfizer & Company?

A: For approximately three years, until about the middle of 1961.

Q: What happened in 1961? What did you do?

A: I changed my position because my wife had been ill and I was forced to get a position that would put me a little closer to home rather than in a territory that was further away, and later in 1961 my wife passed away.

Q: Were there heavy bills and debts that you ran up at that time?

A: Yes, sir. Extremely large ones.

Q: Did you ultimately pay those debts?

A: Yes, sir.

Q: Did you ever resort to any kind of criminal or unlawful or devious activity to pay those debts?

A: No, sir.

Q: Prior to your arrest in this case, had you ever in your life been arrested for anything ever at any time or at any place?

A: No, sir.

Q: In June of 1964 did something happen in your life?

A: In June of 1964 I remarried. I married my present wife, Angelina.

Q: Is your daughter by your first marriage still with the family?

A: Yes, sir, and my present wife has formally adopted my daughter from my first marriage.

Q: Have you had any other children since you were married?

A: Two: a girl and a boy. The girl is now three and a half and my son was two the day before yesterday.

Q: So that you now have three children, is that correct?

A: Yes, sir.

Q: Coming now to September of 1964, did something happen in that month?

A: Yes, sir. In September of 1964 I enrolled as a full-time student at the Columbia Institute of Chiropractic in New York City on West 74th Street.

Q: What was the course that you were taking at the Columbia Institute of Chiropractic?

A: This was a full-time resident course covering a period of either four years or an accelerated program, the one in which I enrolled, which would be three years. This would entail going right through the summer and not having any time off and you would accelerate and receive ultimately your degree of Doctor of Chiropractic, a three-year accelerated program.

Q: Did you ultimately receive a degree?

A: Yes, sir, in September of 1967.

Q: Are you now associated with the institute in any way?

A: Yes, sir. I am an instructor at the Columbia Institute of Chiropractic in the Department of Anatomy and in chiropractic science.

Q: After finishing your education at the Columbia Institute of Chiropractic did you take any licensing examination?

A: Yes, sir. In October of 1967 I took my New Jersey medical board examination and received my license in December of that year, following the examination in October.

Q: You are now duly licensed, I take it?

A: I am duly licensed in New Jersey.

Q: Now going back to 1965, you were at that time a full-time student at the Columbia Institute of Chiropractic, is that correct?

A: Yes, sir.

Q: Were you doing anything else?

A: I was employed full-time by the Metropolitan Life Insurance Company. In October I became employed by the Metropolitan Life Insurance Company.

Q: And what were your duties and responsibilities while you were employed by the Metropolitan?

A: I was employed as an insurance salesman. The actual title that they give is a Metropolitan insurance consultant. This is a salesman of life insurance, and the position that I had was slightly different from the position that the man has who carried the book around with him. I was an insurance consultant with the firm.

Q: Did you have a contract with your company?

A: Yes, sir. On the commencement of employment we did sign a contract which is termed a validation contract.

This is a contract that the agent, or the salesman signs with the company that in effect states that they will pay me a weekly salary in return for which I have to produce so many dollars of insurance production.

This was—should I explain the entire contract?

Q: You might as well.

A: The figures were based on a quarterly basis. My formula to produce insurance was $30,000 of insurance for the first quarter, $50,000 of insurance for the second quarter, and $80,000 for the third quarter, and it continued to graduate up.

In return for this the salary was $450 a month.

Now, when a policy is placed, they use the formula to determine the amount of production that the policy was worth to the individual salesman, and this production had to equal or surpass the amount that had to be written for the quarter, whatever the figures happened to be.

Q: Now, in fact, though, sir, when you sell a life insurance policy, people aren't required to pay the full annual premium at once, and in fact often don't do so. Is that right?

A: That's true.

Q: In other words, some people say they will pay quarterly and other people say they will pay at different intervals, right?

A: Right, sir.

Q: Now, you began working for the life insurance company in October of '65. Is that correct?

A: That's correct.

Q: Now, at that time were you using your income as a salesman to help support your family while you were going to school?

A: Yes, sir.

Q: And was your wife also bringing in money?

A: Yes, sir.

Q: In August of '66 did she—did the money stop coming in from her because she was pregnant?

A: That's right. The baby was born in September of '66.

Q: So that in September of '66 the burden, the full burden and impact and responsibility of supporting your family was now on you and you alone, is that correct?

A: Yes, sir.

Q: Which was as it should be, is that right?

A: That's right.

Q: You were also a full-time student, is that right?

A: Right.

Q: Now, what significance did your position have to you, your position with the life insurance company?

A: It was most important. First of all, it was the type of position
that would allow me to have flexible enough hours to attend
school full-time and also study.

At the same time, it was something that gave me a
guarantee of a weekly income so that I did have the income.

Of what other importance is a position? I could not at that
point be unemployed. It was a most important position to
me.

Q: Now, were you ever tempted by the pressures of your
situation to turn to any form of criminal activity? For
example, passing counterfeit money?

A: No, sir.

Q: Or any other kind of criminal activity?

A: No, sir.

Q: Were there any pressures associated with your job on you?

A: Unfortunately this is probably the only bad feature of the
position, is that there was constantly a lot of pressure to
produce at least the minimum that I had to produce in
order to continue to be paid.

Q: When you say pressure, what do you mean?

A: A salesman is pushed by his manager, and it makes your life
a little bit miserable sometimes, but you are constantly
pushed by your manager.

In addition, in my particular situation at this time he was
on my back, and I guess that's reasonable. His manager is
on his back. If I don't produce that amount of insurance for
a particular quarter I was in jeopardy, my job was in
jeopardy.

Q: Did they ever make it clear that if for any reason you didn't
produce that you might have to start thinking about
another job for yourself?

A: These were the terms of the contract. If you didn't reach a
figure, you could be let go.

Q: And at the very least they would take you off a salary?

A: It was never put to me that way, but I guess at the very least
that was a possibility.

Q: Now assuming that somebody didn't pay their premium

when it came up, what did the policy provide with respect to what happened to the policy?

A: It would lapse after a grace period of thirty days. It would lapse.

Q: Whose responsibility, under your company's rules and procedures, was it to go out and collect a premium when it was overdue and didn't come in?

A: When a premium was not paid it was my responsibility as the salesman, as it is the servicing agent, also to collect that premium. I had to try to have the premium paid.

Q: Did there ever come a time when you were introduced to somebody named Dominick Caputo?

A: Yes, sir. We were introduced by a co-student of mine who was at the time working for Mr. Caputo.

Q: And when did this happen?

A: In the neighborhood of April of 1966.

Q: What was your purpose in being introduced to Mr. Caputo?

A: My friend, my co-student, thought that I could probably sell him a policy on his life, on Mr. Caputo's life.

Q: What was the final outcome with respect to your efforts to sell an insurance to Mr. Caputo?

A: I did sell a policy to Mr. Caputo, and the policy was issued beginning June 1, 1966. The policy was issued to Mr. Caputo at that time.

Q: Do you remember how much the face amount of the policy was?

A: Yes, sir. $35,000.

Q: Do you recall what the annual premium was?

A: In the neighborhood of $1,700 a year, $1,600 a year.

Q: Did Mr. Caputo pay the full annual premium?

A: No, sir. The policy originally was issued on a semi-annual basis, and when we actually put it into effect it was made to be paid quarterly, four times a year. So that's what the policy was. Four times a year it was to be paid.

Q: What happened when the second installment came due?

A: I was notified by the company that it hadn't been paid.

Q: When you received notification that Mr. Caputo had not paid the second premium, what did you do, if anything?

A: I immediately contacted him by phone, and set up a meeting for me to see him in person to attempt to collect the premium at that time.

Q: What happened?

A: I explained the situation of what would happen, that after a thirty-day grace period the policy would go into a situation that we called lapsed, it would become out of effect, and he would endanger his policy. He indicated he wanted to keep the policy, and he indicated that money was a little bit tight for him, and he would be getting monies back from his job. He was constructing pools at this time. He would be getting monies from his jobs and he would pay his premium within the next few days and he would mail it into the office. That is in effect what had happened at the meeting.

Q: And what happened in a few days?

A: We didn't receive the premium. I again called him, and told him that it was supposed to have been in the mail, he had promised it and we were coming now close to the end of his grace period, and what did he intend to do and he said he would mail the check out, he would mail in the premium.

Q: What happened then?

A: He didn't mail in the premium. And now we are to the time that the policy would lapse.

I called him and we set up a meeting again at one of his job sites.

Savarese went on to describe the growing pressures he felt. If the Caputo policy lapsed, he would be headed for deep financial trouble. He had already received credit for a full year's premiums which he would have to make up by selling a new policy for the same amount. And new sales were getting more and more difficult to come by. All of which meant that there was a good chance he would lose his job. Finding a new job offering the flexible hours he needed so he could go to college would be very difficult.

Joe and his wife agreed that it was vital for him to keep the policy in force, in order to protect his job. So, in desperation, Joe offered to lend Caputo $300 towards the premium.

This did save Savarese's job but, as he was soon to discover, it was a strictly temporary solution.

Q: What happened with respect to the money you had loaned him?

A: I called him about four days after I lent him the money because he had said that the money would be available in approximately three or four days. I hadn't heard from him, and I didn't receive the money, so I called him and he said that he didn't have the money yet but he would, in the very near future, again have the money.

I didn't get the money. I called a couple of times, he called a couple of times. We set up a meeting, he cancelled the meeting. This was going on over a period of months. This was through August of 1966 and September of '66. This was a very bad time.

Q: Did there come a time when the third premium became due on the Caputo policy?

A: Yes, sir. That premium was to be paid in December.

I had been, I would say, in constant contact between the date of the second premium and the third premium because of the difficulty I had had with the second premium.

Q: Now, Mr. Savarese, what happened when the third premium on the Caputo policy became due?

A: I, prior to the due date of the third premium, began to literally hound him for the premium before the time of the due date because of the fact that we had so much trouble with the second premium.

At this point we also had—I also had the situation that he owed me money, too, from the second premium. So I began to be in constant touch with him from the time that I lent him the money and the first call a few days after that until the time that this whole thing came about, which would be in November.

Q: Did it ever occur to you at this time that Mr. Caputo was perhaps manipulating you a little bit?

A: In this period? Yes, sir.

Q: Did Mr. Caputo pay his third premium?

A: No, sir.

Q: What, if anything, did you do to try to get Mr. Caputo to pay the premium, the third premium?

A: I called him many, many, many times.

Q: Did you ever go to see him in person?

A: Yes, sir.

Q: How many times, about?

A: There was a period of about three weeks there that I must have seen him almost every day because he was working at a job in Rye, New York, which was very close to me, and I was over there almost every day for a period of about two weeks. This would be the end of October, early November.

Q: Did there come a time when Mr. Caputo came up with an unusual idea for solving the problem?

A: Yes, sir.

Q: How did he actually bring the subject up?

A: It was probably—we were having coffee, and he said that— the first time he brought it up he just asked almost out of the blue, had I ever been approached for the purchase of counterfeit money, or to buy counterfeit money.

The second time, which would probably be a day or two later because I was seeing him almost every day to try to collect the money, and I figured if I'm there when he gets the checks from his customers, that's the only way I was going to get my premium and the money he owed us.

But over coffee, this was the second time he brought this up, he said that if I had again been approached for any counterfeit money and if I hadn't it was too bad that I couldn't have a contact for him because he has a means of disposing of large amounts of counterfeit money if he could get his hands on it.

I told him it was ridiculous, the whole idea is ridiculous to do anything with counterfeit money, and I let it drop there.

Q: Did you know of any source of counterfeit money? Could you have laid your hands on counterfeit money if you had wanted to?

A: No, sir.

Q: Did you tell him that?

A: Yes, I told him very definitely.

Q: What was his reaction when you said that?

A: He said that this fellow who worked for him told him that that area was so bad, that the area was bad, and Mr. Caputo at one time had a girl friend on 72nd Street on the West Side, and apparently these things were done. Counterfeit money was bought, dope was bought, stolen, this or that or everything, and almost anything you could manage at one time or another you could be approached for if you are in that area enough, and he knew that I was in that area every night for five hours going to school.

He said, "Come on, you know that there are people around there selling counterfeit money."

Frankly, I didn't know that there were people selling counterfeit money in that area.

Q: Did there come a time when you finally agreed to help him out?

A: I would say he finally convinced me to the fact that getting him a name, I would not involve myself. I originally thought the idea, as I said, was foolish. I didn't want the involvement. Eventually it seemed, well, by getting him the name of a person, I am not involving myself, just by getting him a name.

So what I subsequently did was ask a friend, another co-student who worked in a restaurant in that area, a Ham & Egg Restaurant on West 71st Street, he was a manager there. I asked him if he ever had contact in the store with anybody who dealt in counterfeit money.

Q: What was your discussion with your friend? What did you say to him?

A: I told him that I was uptight with the job. I told him the situation. I told him that one of my policyholders had asked me if I could find him a contact to purchase counterfeit money.

My friend told me I was crazy. He said leave yourself out of it. He said no, don't even bother.

Although with many misgivings, Savarese's friend did eventually manage to set up an appointment with Nino, a restaurant regular, who was suspected of being a supplier of counterfeit money. Let's pick up the story as Joe digs himself in deeper and deeper.

Q: So that at the time you were going to meet this fellow, did you yourself know, in fact, whether he was a dealer in counterfeit money or just some guy who happened perhaps even unwittingly to have a bad bill that he passed?

A: I didn't know.

Q: Tell us about that. Did you have a meeting with this fellow?

A: Caputo was supposed to meet him, but he more or less weaseled me into going. He said that he couldn't make the meeting the next day with this guy . . . He said, "All you have to do is just find out if he's got the bills."

So I did make the meeting. I argued with him a little but I did make the meeting because I was going to be down there at school at 6 o'clock. So I made the meeting for 5:30.

Q: What was the gist of the meeting?

A: He said that he did have money for sale, and Caputo had specifically been interested in amounts of $10,000 to be increased later, and he said he did have $10,000 for sale, and he gave me what the price would be, which I believe was $36 to $38 a hundred for the bad bills.

Q: Did you set another meeting?

A: The same place at approximately the same time. I would say it was about a week or four days later.

Q: Now, did you indicate to Nino that you would be there or that Caputo would be there?

A: Caputo would be there.

Q: What was the next thing that happened with respect to Caputo and you and Nino?

A: When I got home that night, Caputo had called. He was very reliable on his calls when he wanted something, it seems. He had called and my wife told me that he had called and I called him back because he was very anxious to hear what happened, and I told him that he did have the money for sale, he did have an amount of $10,000, and the price, the time, and the place that he was to meet him, and then I told him that that is it, out.

I made that meeting much against my better judgment. I told him I was scared. I felt terrible standing there on the corner with this guy who's got counterfeit money and I was worried, and I told him so, and I told him that I had had it and that was the last thing. I more than fulfilled my original statement that I would get him a name. . . .

Q: Now, after this, what happened?

A: It was the night before the date of the meeting which I had forgotten about completely because I was not involved, and again I got home from school, and there was a call from Caputo, and I called him back, and he said he wanted to see me in the morning. He had some money for me.

When I got there that morning, there was no premium for me so I was up there on a ruse just to get me there.

And when I got there, he said that he had an appointment with a town council in New Paltz, New York, to give them figures and an estimate on rebuilding the high school pool there, and it would be impossible for him to make the meeting.

Q: What was your reaction to this?

A: So what? I really didn't suspect that he was going to ask me the next question—to make the meeting for him.

Q: What was your answer when he asked you to make the meeting for him? What was your reaction?

A: To say I got angry was to say the least because I was angry already when I found out he didn't have the premium money that I was coming for. And then I really became steamed. And I started to walk away. He ran after me, and we talked a while at the car, but I refused. I couldn't do anything like that, and I won't show up at a meeting like this. I said, "Just don't go and maybe you can arrange another meeting."

And he said no, that the people that he had made a deal with to get rid of the money, would cancel out if he didn't deliver the money that night or tomorrow, whenever he was supposed to deliver it. And I just said too bad. At this point, you know, if everything depends on you paying my premium, let the premium go, forget it. I can't get involved anymore.

I was still in bad shape so far as the job was concerned and he knew it, and he brought this out to my attention again and he is giving me, well, what are you doing? All you are going to have to do is show up. And he took out a pile of bills, good money. "I will give you the money and just go down. You are a messenger; you are not involved."

I told him no, I wouldn't do this.

Q: What was the next thing that happened?

A: He talked me into it. He buffaloed me into it, or however you want to call it. By the time we finished the conversation I was mad. I was very mad. I was also getting more worried now because of the fact that he just put up in my face all the things that I know of my situation and how bad it was and he talked me into making the meeting that night and he gave me the money. He gave me somewhere in the neighborhood of $1,900 to make the exchange with this guy and to tell him that he would have the rest of the money and buy the other half of it because he only had enough for half of it.

It must have been $36 a hundred. He had only money for half of the original amount that he was going to buy from him, which was $10,000. At any rate, he gave me the money. And that was in the late morning. And that night at 5:30 I did make a meeting with Nino at 71st Street and Broadway in front of the restaurant.

Q: This was your second meeting with Nino, is that correct?

A: Yes, sir.

Q: And was it at this second meeting that you exchanged good money for bad?

A: Yes, sir.

Q: Whose good money was it?

A: Caputo's or whoever he had borrowed it from.

Q: Was any of that good money that you exchanged, your money?

A: Not a dime.

Q: What did you receive in return?

A: He gave me a bag—well, we met, and he had me drive around the block. I would say he was as scared as I was, and I was very scared. My teeth were chattering. Well, Caputo said I wasn't involved, but I was scared. I was really scared.

Q: You knew you were breaking the law, didn't you?

A: Well, not really that I was breaking the law because I wasn't involved. I wasn't to receive anything monetarily from this, so I was not—maybe on the outside fringe of breaking the law. I was a messenger. In effect, I was doing nothing else and I didn't really feel that I was doing something wrong, but I knew I was going to get the counterfeit money and what happened if I had an accident on the way home and this stuff is laying all over my car? I was worried. Anyhow, I took the bag and gave him the good money. He didn't count it. Which surprised me. He just went flip through the bills that were wrapped in a rubber band, got out of the car and took off, and that was the extent of the meeting.

Q: Did you count the counterfeit money?

A: Not then. Caputo counted it the next morning. But before he had a chance to do anything when I got out of the car I was screaming at him for what he had—I just told him in a couple of minutes my whole feelings from the night before. What if I had gotten into an accident with all this money in the car?

Q: What happened then?

A: He wanted me to take some of the money back, or return it.

Q: Why did he want you to return it?

A: He said it was bad. Some of it was very bad, and—well, I will agree with that. It was all very bad.

Q: What was the next thing that happened? What did you say when he asked you to—when he told you about wanting you to have the money taken back, what did you say to that?

A: I told him definitely no. I am finished. I have had it. This has gone much, much further than I—I knew I had made a mistake, and I had had it. Definitely no. No more contact whatsoever with this. If you pay me your premium fine, if you don't pay me your premium fine. Just leave me alone. If you have got to lapse your policy, lapse your policy. I said, "If you want to return it, you return it." I told him there was a date set up because he wanted an additional $10,000 and this was the situation. And so I told him if he wants to meet him to buy another $10,000 worth, he can exchange the money himself then, and I told him the date of the meeting which was November 28.

Q: Now, what was the next contact that you had with Caputo? Incidentally, did Caputo give you anything? Did he pay you anything, either good money or bad money for what you had done for him?

A: No payment for what I had done for him and no payment on his premium.

Q: Did you have any counterfeit money in your possession after you had given it to him? Did you keep any of it?

A: No, sir.

Q: Did you ever try to pay for anything with a counterfeit bill?

A: No, sir.

Q: What happened next? What was the next contact you had with Caputo?

A: November 27, the day before he was to meet Nino, which again I didn't put any—

Q: You say November 27. Is this the day before the day when you were finally arrested by federal agents?

A: Right.

Q: What was the contact?

A: A phone call when I got home from school. There was a call that Caputo had called and I called him. And he was very nice on the phone. And he said that he was sorry for all the trouble he caused, and all the aggravation he gave me, and his deal had gone through and he will pay his premium. And to come up in the morning. And again I went back to Rye in the morning.

Q: How many days did he have left to pay the premium before the policy went?

A: It was not in danger of lapse at that time, not on this

premium. This was the premium I was hounding him be-fore that was due. It was due on December 1st. This was November 28th.

Q: Did you in fact go up and see him on the morning of November 28.

A: Yes, sir. At the job in Rye. I saw him I'd say probably about 11 o'clock. When I got there he said—he started to explain that he didn't have the premium but it was coming because I immediately started to boil. But he said it was coming.

He said he got, he had gotten money from a friend, I think he said a friend in Yonkers who was going to give him the money to buy the additional $10,000 of bad money that night, and he would be able to give me the money when he met this guy. This guy was going with him to the meeting. This guy turned out to be the Secret Service man. . . .

So I said, "Well, why did you get me up here for this? It seems silly." I probably cursed at him. Because at this point he dragged me up there and—for nothing. If he had to tell me that he was going to have the money that night, he could have told me that on the phone. Or if he wanted to call me that night and tell me he had the money, then fine. So you will pay the premium one day later. One day wouldn't make that much difference. I probably did curse at him.

Q: What else did Mr. Caputo say?

A: He asked me to do him a favor. He said that they wouldn't be able to identify this fellow Nino, so I described him again for him and I said, "You will have no trouble whatsoever because he is very dark, dark hair, dark eyes, dark complex-ion and he wears a trench coat like you see in the movies. No problem whatsoever identifying this fellow."

He said, "Well, could you do me a favor and just point him out to us?"

So I told him no. I didn't want to be anywhere around. It's bad enough I had to be at school which was a block away about the time they were supposed to have the meeting. I told him no . . . So after I argued with him that I didn't want to be involved, he said, "Look, I'm meeting him. All you have to do is point him out and that's the whole thing."

And he was going to do the whole thing himself. So we arranged a meeting for 4:30 that night . . .

Now, he asked me if—he said that he didn't want to run around all day with the [counterfeit] money. He had no place to keep the $6,000 that he wanted to bring back to Nino. So he had no place to put it, and I guess not, because he was in work clothes. He had nowhere to put it.

He didn't want to meet this fellow to pick up the money in Yonkers with the counterfeit money on him, and not being able to put it anywhere he asked me if I would hold it until we met at 4:30.

I argued, but it didn't seem like a problem. It was reasonable. After I argued a little bit, so I carried the money down for him to meet him at 4:30 so that they could go meet Nino.

Q: Now, did you, in fact, go to the meeting that Caputo had told you about?

A: I, in fact, went to the meeting, I met him at 4:30 at 72nd Street and West End Avenue.

Q: What happened then?

A: I met him at the drugstore. He introduced me to his friend, who I later found out was the agent. He introduced me to his friend, and we walked over to the car.

I conversed with Caputo some. I didn't talk to his friend at all, but I will say that the minute I saw the car I became petrified.

Q: Why?

A: This fellow was supposed to be a friend from Yonkers, and there was a big 5K plate on that car, and K is—that's Brooklyn.

Q: What does K stand for on a license plate, as far as you know?

A: Brooklyn. Kings County.

Q: Did you say anything to him?

A: The only words I had with the agent were hello in front of the drugstore. When we got into the car I spoke to Caputo and I said almost nothing to the agent. I was afraid of him. I was afraid of this car, and I was consequently afraid of him, and I wasn't talking to him. Caputo and I did the talking.

Q: Did Caputo ask you if you had the money?

A: He did ask me that.

Q: What did you say when he asked you that?

A: You know I have it.

Q: What happened then?

A: The agent said something like, "How much does it cost?"

He said something to the effect that he was going to buy this from me, and I really panicked.

Q: What happened then?

A: Caputo said, "Do you have the money with you?" I said yes again. He knew that I had the money. He had given it to me that morning. And he said, "Let me see."

I gave him—I opened my bag and whatever I grabbed, the two packs, I guess, two packs to Caputo. The agent grabbed it, and he said that he had the money in the car, and he got out of the car and that's when the arrest took place. There were agents all around the car pointing guns at me and they said "You are under arrest."

Q: What did you do?

A: I started crying.

What had happened was, of course, fairly evident. Caputo had been arrested while trying to pass the phony bills and the Secret Service agents had got him to set up Joe Savarese.

The agents took Savarese down to their offices and, after he signed a statement for them, gave him a similar proposition to the one they had given to Caputo. They wanted Joe to help them get Nino and through him the printing plant where the counterfeit money was produced.

Savarese agreed, and for many weeks he worked with the agents looking for Nino, chasing down leads and suggesting ideas. After a while, he began socializing with the agents and pretty soon he began to feel like a Secret Service man himself. All this while, he was completely free. He had never been arraigned. And no bail had ever been set. There was never any hint that he had anything to fear.

The search for Nino was unsuccessful and after a couple of

years the agents decided that they had milked their cow dry. The boom came down with a bang. Savarese, who had set up a practice and was accepted and even honored in his community, got the shock of his life. Out of a clear sky he was indicted and arrested and, while his head was still spinning, put on trial before a judge and jury. The agents with whom he had been so chummy turned cold and distant.

At the trial, Caputo—who, it turned out, had had a few earlier brushes with the law—testified against Savarese. The jury found him guilty. The judge sentenced him to one year—six months in prison and six months on probation. Caputo, who had previously pleaded guilty, got only six months.

The Secret Service agents probably felt justified in their actions. Their job as they saw it was to track down the higher-ups in the counterfeiting ring and shut them down. In the process I felt that they treated Savarese shabbily. They got his complete and enthusiastic cooperation. They worked with him as though he were one of them. And then, when he least expected it, they helped land him in jail.

In his cell, Savarese had plenty of time to ponder his own considerable frailty. And perhaps he learned to suspect the motives of slippery types like Caputo and devious types like certain Secret Service agents.

SEVENTEEN

Cast of Characters
The Client

PEOPLE frequently ask a criminal lawyer whether he feels any fear of the rough characters he meets every day of his working life. After all, violence is second nature to some of these thugs. If they happen to take a dislike to their lawyer, why wouldn't they administer the same treatment to him that they would to anyone else in their line of work?

It's true, in this case, that familiarity breeds contempt. Having known so many holdup men, it's tempting for me to believe that if I met one on the street plying his trade, I would be unafraid and might even try to dissuade him from his purpose.

However, I imagine that, faced with a real, live stickup artist who meant business, I would meekly hand over my wallet with a minimum of fuss. And I certainly would not make it known that I am a criminal lawyer. He might not happen to admire members of that profession.

As clients, criminals don't worry me at all. In my experience, most of them are in awe of their lawyer. Whatever he does is fine with them. Should they go to prison, they usually feel that their lawyer did everything possible and that they would have been a lot worse off without him.

Having said this, I am reminded of one client who did become quite hostile, to put it mildly. He was a big, powerful man. I had managed to get him what I considered a fair deal, in light of his extensive record of assaults to go with his one attempted murder. I had pleaded him guilty to simple assault and got him a year in the workhouse. He could easily have drawn a ten-year sentence.

A month or so passed and one day I received a letter from him written in the workhouse. He demanded his money back, saying that if he didn't get it, I would live to be sorry. He had a forceful, if overly vivid writing style, and managed to convey his plans for me—should the money not be forthcoming—in plain, unmistakable language. The letter of course could not have passed the workhouse authorities. It had been kited out—that is, a workhouse employee or a visitor had taken it out and mailed it uncensored from the outside.

I paid no attention to the letter. The next month a second one arrived. This was equally explicit. One of the memorable sentences ran, "When I get out, this city will not be big enough for you and me. I will find you—at your office or at your home." Month after month, the letters continued to arrive, while I grew steadily more uneasy.

One day, I found myself discussing the matter with the district attorney. I asked him whether he thought I should get a pistol permit and buy a pistol to go with it. He laughed and said that I would probably shoot myself in the leg the first day I got it.

It was a quiet day, I recall, and I was reading a brief in my office when my secretary came in and announced our friend, recently released from the workhouse.

"Send him in," I said with very little enthusiasm.

My ex-client appeared huge in the doorway. "Mr. Roth-blatt," he said, "could you lend me a dollar?"

I have seldom before reached so quickly for my pocket. I handed over the dollar and then ventured a question. "Jones, why did you send me all those letters asking for your money back?"

Jones smiled. "You can't blame a fellow for trying," he said.

A criminal lawyer knows better than anyone, except for the criminals themselves, that crime does not pay—literally. One of my former clients estimated that the net return on his assorted crimes, taking into account the time spent in jail, came to five dollars a day. Even the dumbest of criminals, and some are moronic indeed, can understand that they are playing a losing game. To many, unfortunately, the realization comes too late.

Ironically, some crooks land in jail because of their beginner's luck. Their first job pans out and they feel richer by a few hundred or even a few thousand dollars. How long has this been going on, they wonder gleefully, as they plan the next job. But the euphoria doesn't last. Soon there's the inevitable awakening. Like horse players, they're destined to end up broke—and what's more, locked up.

Occasionally, a hardened offender will make up his mind to go straight. And he will for a while. Until one day when he can no longer resist the temptation for one last big "score." Then, with all that nice money, he will retire to a life of comfort and respectability. No more policemen hounding him, no more lousy jailhouse food, no more guns pointed at him.

That's not the way it works out. Instead something goes wrong. Is it fate, accident, or what that causes his downfall? In any case, back to jail he goes.

In my time, I have known many "perfect crimes" that were thwarted by unpredictable events and one-chance-in-a-million coincidences. Is there an unseen hand at work? Some of these developments are so strange that you wonder. Here is an example:

Two gentlemen from out of town came to New York on orders to take a rival racketeer "for a ride" in typical gangland style. They selected what seemed to be an ideal spot for the event—a lonely, almost deserted area in the northeast Bronx. In fact, there was only one house within a hundred yards of the spot where they "rubbed out" their victim.

Now the eerie part of the story. What the two mobsters had no way of knowing was that in that very house there lived a father and son, both detectives in the New York City Police Homicide Squad!

The killers' shots rang out. The two detectives, both at home at the time, were hot on the trail in less than a minute. The chase was short and eventful, and the luckless pair wound up serving appropriately long terms in jail.

One reason the run-of-the-mill crook turns to crime is that he is not intelligent enough to hold even a poorly paid job. Some convicts actually have tried to make it in the normal world, only to become disheartened when they fail to measure up. These are the people that deserve our sympathy. I wish our society could make room for them.

Such misfits have all the desires and needs of the rest of us, but no way of earning the money to satisfy these needs. In desperation they turn to something they can do—slug some luckless pedestrian and take his wallet, or break into a store or apartment. That some of them get away with it for a while is no tribute to their cleverness. It merely indicates that there are just not enough policemen to go around.

One safecracker client of mine surprised me one day with a demonstration of dumbness that was unusual even for a criminal. He was out on bail and worried about his upcoming trial. He called me in a somber mood. "Mr. Rothblatt, do you think I ought to L-A-M?" he said. I was puzzled for a moment. Then I realized that he was spelling out "lam," gangster slang for leave town, jump bail. In his mind, I suppose, he was cleverly confusing anyone who might be listening in.

"No, George," I told him. "Don't L-A-M."

There are of course many other reasons to explain criminal behavior. Laziness—the sheer resistance to getting out of bed and to the job—accounts for some careers in crime. Mental disorders are behind many others—producing warped personalities including sociopaths who get their kicks out of hurting others.

Even relatively normal defendants, facing a major charge, tend to become paranoid. The press has a disturbing practice that helps to induce this condition. When there are several indictments, or a lot of counts in a single indictment, the reporter neatly totes up all the punishments involved and informs his readers that the defendant is facing a sentence of 150 years in prison.

This may be technically true, but it never happens. In almost every case where there are convictions on multiple counts, the sentences run concurrently, not consecutively.

Instead of 150 years, the defendant may actually do only two or three.

Doctors tell me that one of their biggest headaches comes from patients who prefer the information given in an article they read about their ailment to that supplied by the doctor. This happens to lawyers, too. I have often been greeted by a terrified client, wildly waving a newspaper clipping about his case. I tell him not to worry. My shoulders are broad enough to carry the whole load, and more. "I will do everything for you," I say, "Except serve your time." For some reason, this little joke never gets a laugh.

Above all, the criminal lawyer has to listen to his client, not just look as though he is listening. He must get all the facts. The one he misses could make all the difference. An example:

A lawyer friend had a client who was charged with statutory rape (intercourse with a woman under eighteen.) The client denied the charge but could think of no way to prove his innocence.

Just before the trial, the client happened to mention that he had had an operation on his prostate. It turned out that the operation was performed shortly before the alleged rape took place. He could not possibly have had intercourse when charged, a fact that was confirmed by the doctors who treated him.

Defense counsel simply cannot rely on a client to remember all pertinent details—or to mention them if he should remember. It's up to the lawyer to cross-examine his client even more thoroughly than he does a hostile witness on the stand.

Most blue-collar defendants, charged with run-of-the-mill crimes, are easy to get along with. If they lose, they usually take it philosophically. Not so white-collar defendants. A businessman is used to giving orders. He tells the lawyer what to do. If you give him advice before the indictment, he may claim that you are responsible for his difficulties. If he should be convicted, watch out.

In white-collar crimes, it is often hard to know whether the defendant actually intended to steal, forge, embezzle, or whatever. Perhaps he simply made an innocent mistake.

To dramatize this point in court, I keep a careful record of all the times during the trial that the judge rules against something that the prosecutor says or does. Then, in my summation, I am able to say to the jury, "In exactly twenty-four [or thirty-nine or seventy-seven, as the case may be] instances during this trial, the judge decided that the prosecutor was wrong. The prosecutor did not mean to deceive you; his were honest mistakes, not crimes. The same is true of my much more ignorant, less sophisticated client."

This can be an effective argument and very often it fairly explains what actually happened. For instance, a few years ago, Deputy Attorney General William D. Ruckelshaus brought a young Finnish woman into the United States to work in his household without realizing he had violated the immigration laws. Nor is Ruckelshaus alone among prominent lawyers in his confusion. Lee Bailey, who has represented many white-collar defendants, considers the U.S. Postal Service one of the most dangerous government departments to tangle with. That is so because of the complex mail-fraud statutes. Lee says that these laws, taken together, constitute a "shotgun" that can blow your brains out when you least expect it. Pretty soon, moreover, lots of other agencies—as many as six—get into the act, some not knowing about the others, and you begin to feel like a character in a Kafka novel.

Anyone who spends a week in my office will leave convinced that the sex drive is powerful indeed. In will come a married man or woman insane with jealousy and primed for murder, a woman or man planning to charge a rival or lover with adultery or seduction. More often, it is an ordinary-looking young man who has committed a sex crime for which he will pay in endless shame—a ruined career, and a prison term staring him in the face.

Sometimes the sex instinct, when thwarted, takes bizarre forms. I recall going to a local jail to see a man transferred from an upstate prison where he had served seven years for armed robbery. His release was now imminent.

As I spoke with him, his eyes suddenly opened wide and his

head swiveled to follow the figure of a woman employee passing through. The woman was elderly, dumpy of figure and plain of face—not the type to arouse. Yet, to look at the prisoner's face, you would have thought that he was watching Miss America.

I must confess that my mind was uneasy as I watched this convict's reaction to the woman in the jailhouse. It occurred to me that maybe there was something to be said for the Mexican system of allowing conjugal visits by wives or girlfriends to men serving long terms.

At this point, let me tell you about a few of my clients who don't appear elsewhere in this book. I include them because they are strange, interesting, instructive or typical.

Glenn Turner, the dynamic business promoter, was under investigation by a grand jury for alleged fraud in one of his ingenious enterprises, which the government thought was a bit too ingenious. Lee Bailey and I, acting for him, sent him in to testify. He held the grand jury spellbound for forty-five minutes and they all but gave him a standing ovation when he was through.

Among Turner's gems: "I never got beyond the sixth grade, and what I have I got by hard work. I'm trying to get people off relief and have them put in an honest day's work." The grand jury, all solid citizens, loved it. My partner, Steve Peskin, told me, "If I had five more minutes with him, I'd quit the law and throw in with him. He's like a giant magnet."

A prosperous businessman I represented was entertained by a highly qualified lady of the evening. On leaving her tasteful pad, he was pounced on by a couple of lurking cops.

"Where did you leave the hash?" they yelled as they slammed him against the wall and slipped on the handcuffs.

Practically fainting from fear, my client stammered that he was not a dope peddler, he had only been having a good time.

The cops had no good reason not to believe him. So to avoid a total loss, they took him in for patronizing a prostitute, a charge I had no trouble beating before a male-chauvinist-pig judge.

A year and a half later, my client got a chilling call from the IRS. (All calls from the IRS are chilling.) They wanted to know how much he had paid the prostitute. Seems they suspected her of shortchanging the tax collector.

There wasn't any big hassle involved but throughout my chat with the Feds, I kept visualizing good old Uncle Sam reaching out for his cut of the whore's take—just like those well-dressed gentlemen who ride around in their gold-colored Cadillacs.

A man I didn't know walked into my office and put down a retainer. "I thought maybe I should have a lawyer," he said.

"Anything bad?" I asked.

"Just a fight in a bar."

"Anybody hurt?"

"Just one guy dead and another wounded."

I stared at him but he was quite serious. In his circles, this was just a minor misunderstanding. He and his friends are masters of euphemism. People aren't killed, they are "knocked off" or "rubbed out." The Russians called murder liquidation; to the Nazis, it was the final solution.

The fact that Bernard Barker was shot down and imprisoned by the Nazis and that several of the other Watergate "Cubans" had excellent war records would have been a big plus for our defense in the break-in case, had that case gone to trial. The average juror feels that the nation owes a war veteran special consideration, especially if he was wounded or decorated. The juror also tends to believe that the defendant's personality may have been warped by his war experiences and that he deserves a break.

A lawyer acquaintance recently told me about a client of his who, every year, claimed $4,500 as a charitable-contribution deduction. This was the maximum—15 percent of income—allowed at the time. His tax form said that he gave the money to his church.

After this had gone on for a few years, the IRS computers got suspicious. The result was a call from the tax people suggesting a review of the large deduction. The client promptly produced a batch of checks made out to the church for amounts totaling more than $4,500! Abashed, the IRS snoopers withdrew.

Later, the client confided to his lawyer that he was a church official and that every Sunday, after all the basket contributions were counted, he would take the cash and give the church treasurer his own check in that amount. These were the checks he showed the IRS.

Whenever he tells this story, everyone laughs heartily. Why, my lawyer friend wonders, do so many people like to see the tax collectors foiled?

Advice to young defendants from a judge:

It is not a good idea for a youth to show up in court in a skivvy shirt, a leather jacket and long hair. A judge, like everyone else, goes by appearances. A kid who says "Yes, sir," and "No, sir," instead of "Yeah," may save himself a prison term. Also, the presence of parents in the courtroom and a letter from a former teacher can make all the difference.

But more than anything else is the almighty job. We judges love workers and hate loafers. We all believe devoutly that the devil makes work for idle hands.

This next fellow wasn't my brainiest client, or the nicest— and certainly not the handsomest. But he was easily the luckiest. Read on.

Charles Russell, a Bronx restaurant cook, drew a prison sentence of three to six years for assaulting a man named Glorian Ferguson, in 1954. Russell had planted a bullet near Ferguson's spine. In self-defense, he said.

Now, the injury was so serious that there was a chance that Ferguson might die, which would put Russell in deep trouble. So when the district attorney and the judge offered him a deal, he accepted. The agreement was that if Russell pleaded guilty, the case would be closed. After he served his time, he could forget all about the unhappy event.

Russell served his term with time off for good behavior and was released.

In 1959, he once again indulged his propensity for violence and was sentenced as a second offender to seven and a half to twenty years on a plea of guilty to robbery in the third degree.

Russell was still serving time in 1964 when fate suddenly stepped in. Ferguson, the man Russell shot, died. The medical examiner reported that death was due to the bullet—so near the spine that doctors had feared to remove it.

At this point, the district attorney decided to get into the act. Since Ferguson died of the bullet fired by Russell, he reasoned, then Russell was guilty of murder. With the excess zeal typical of some D.A.s, he proceeded to have Russell indicted for murder in the first degree. At this stage in the proceedings, I was assigned by the court to defend Russell.

This was indeed a strange legal tangle I was thrown into. Russell had originally pleaded guilty on the assurance that his sentence for assault would end the matter once and for all. Ten years later, the D.A. reneged and charged him with first-degree murder. The courts take a dim view of such tactics by D.A.s. And to complicate things, Russell had already served his time on the Ferguson matter and was in jail for an unrelated offense.

My reaction to all this ran along these lines:

Since Russell was now indicted for murder, the original assault plea and sentence would have to be set aside. Otherwise, Russell would be tried at two different times for two different aspects of the same crime.

Taking it a step further: If the assault plea was set aside, then Russell was not a second offender when convicted of the robbery. So his seven-and-a-half-to-twenty-year-sentence would have to be reduced. And, since he had already spent a long stretch in prison on this sentence, he would have to be freed. So all we had to worry about was the murder indictment.

Events don't always conform closely to a blueprint. But in

this case, everything worked out as planned. The courts set aside the original assault plea on a writ of *coram nobis* (withdrawing a plea after sentencing) and sliced Russell's prison sentence for robbery, which was based on the now-mistaken assumption that he was a second offender. Russell pleaded guilty to manslaughter in the first degree.

In view of the time he had already served for the assault, he received a suspended sentence. In short, he walked away a free man. And all because Ferguson had died at the right moment and the district attorney combined overzealousness with stupidity.

In spite of everything, the Lanes were a loyal, loving couple. Dolly was forty-five and black, Fred some years older, and white. They both loved good food and their figures showed it. Hardly Bonnie and Clyde, but they gave the police of the United States, Canada, and France a lot of headaches. I represented Fred and so got to know Dolly, too.

They were accused of being in the drug business, but maintained they were undercover agents. They were truly split personalities. A lot of the time they seemed to lose track of whether they were working for the cops or for themselves. In this they were not too much different from certain police officers who can't quite make up their minds whether they should arrest drug biggies or just grab the dope and cash as a reward for their fine police work.

The alleged dope-dealing was only one aspect of their lives. Both were used—and abused—by the Federal Bureau of Narcotics, the FBI, and the New York City Bureau of Narcotics—for whom they fingered major drug dealers. Their lives were in continual danger of being snuffed out. Over a period of a few years, more than twenty-five such informers met violent deaths at the hands of the underworld.

In New York City, their center of operations, Dolly and Fred were highly esteemed for ingenuity and nerve. Being black, Dolly could move about Harlem with ease, while Fred was admirably suited for dealing with crooked cops and color-conscious mob types.

Their trouble began at Dorval Airport, outside Montreal in the summer of 1967. Dolly and a companion—not Fred—had just arrived when the Canadian Mounties took two couriers from a Marseilles dope ring into custody. Each had three kilos of heroin strapped around his waist.

Probably on a tip, the Mounties also picked up Dolly and friend and took them in for grilling along with the couriers. While not admitting any connection with the Marseilles men, Dolly did tell the Mounties about previous border-crossing excursions. During one account, she admitted informing a Canadian dope dealer that a mutual acquaintance planned to kill him if he ever showed his face in New York again. She also related the details of impressive Marseilles–Montreal-New York transactions. In all of this, she maintained, she had always acted as an undercover government agent.

Perhaps they believed her. Or maybe a New York narcotics agent at the scene put in a good word for her. In any case the Canadians seemed in a relaxed mood. They merely assigned two Mounties to escort her and her companion to Plattsburg and then firmly point them south.

The two Mounties who got the escort duty were hardly the strong, silent type, as will soon be evident.

Out of the blue one day, Dolly and Fred were picked up and charged with assorted drug offenses. The Mounties, it seems, had been arrested and one of them had decided to talk. His story, convincingly told, involved Dolly and Fred.

At the trial, the Mountie testified:

"Dolly asked if we could take them on a tour of Expo. since it was their last chance to see Expo. We escorted them there, where they stayed approximately an hour and a half. During the evening we became quite friendly and at a point Dolly told us that she was involved in New York in illegal activities such as drugs and fencing."

Apparently the Mounties were not horrified by these revelations. At a cozy $50-for-four dinner that followed (Dolly paid), they held up their end with lively tales of illegal drugs pouring into Canada, much of it brought in by Argentinians eager, likely, to improve their country's image as more than just a beef exporter.

"During the trip," the Mountie went on, "Dolly told us she was very grateful for the way we treated her, because really we were treating her a bit special, and she invited us to New York, you know, and she said if we ever came there she would show us a good time."

The Mounties accepted the invitation. Before many weeks had passed, they were in New York for their promised "good time." They brought with them a sample vial of heroin.

One of the Mounties picked up the story. His testimony:

"Prior to entering the apartment, the vial was in my possession. I took it from the car and I put it in my pocket, and I placed it—between the two elevators there is an ashtray, you know; you lift the top and there is some sand there. I placed that vial right there.

"Well, after a while, we asked if Dolly—if she was serious about what she claimed in Montreal, that she was involved in drugs and stuff and she said that she was serious, and we asked if we had heroin, would she buy it, and she said she would."

So the Canadian retrieved his vial from the ashtray and "She took the vial and smelled it, tasted it, and we argued on the price and we finally agreed on $500 American for the vial."

An astute student of human nature, Dolly supplied a fifty-dollar lady for one of the Mounties—at her expense. The Mounties were charmed by this sample of southern hospitality.

Now that everyone had shown his good faith, talk turned to future deals. A few weeks later, one of the Mounties was back with more heroin—this a bag containing five and a half pounds of it, valued at $27,500.

"We went to their apartment and I saw the money in $5,000 packages. When they took the bag, I held on to my revolver. Now at this point—you know, they saw I had a gun in my hands. I told them that I was afraid of a double cross. They said, 'We are too big and too old in this kind of deal to jeopardize our lives on a rather small deal like this when we have this kind of deal nearly every week.' "

With everybody happy, talk turned to a really big caper. The $27,500 worth had been obtained by the judicious substitution of flour for heroin in the Montreal Royal Canadian Mounted Police Headquarters. The pure stuff had been cut down to 50 percent. (In one of the few light moments of the trial, one Mountie bristled when he thought himself accused of stealing the flour, in addition to his other indiscretions. He protested indignantly that he had bought and paid for it— legitimately.)

Now, the plan concerned heroin kept in the Royal Canadian Mounted Police Headquarters in Ottawa—not to be confused with the Montreal branch. This "could be brought into New York, but we needed somebody to open the safe, so we asked if they could provide us with a safe man.

"We told Dolly we had forty-six kilos that we could get our hands on, and we asked for $10,000 per kilo. We said we were ready to sell them fifty kilos and the remaining six kilos would go to the safe man."

While the safe men were submitting their resumés, the whole project foundered on envy and greed. Mountie #2 asked #1 for his share of the $27,500. He was turned down because he had not made the second trip and had also refused to help with the flour-mixing. Enraged, he went to his bosses with the whole story. Apparently, he had the silly notion that he could convince them that he had merely been trying to trap Mountie #1, just like in the movies. All it got him was ten years in the pen, the same as the other Mountie got.

We put up a good rearguard action and the jury stayed out longer than anyone had expected, but that was cold comfort. Dolly and Fred got fifteen years. The last I heard, they had sworn never to look at another vial of heroin again, foreign or domestic—whether in the government's interest or their own. And they are looking forward eagerly to the day they will be reunited.

A client of mine, a business executive, was called to appear before a grand jury on suspicion of forging checks at a time when his company was being dissolved.

I advised my client to take with him to the hearing every letter, note, memo, and other document bearing on his authority to draw checks.

My client followed my advice with a vengeance. He appeared at the hearing with a great stack of paper and proceeded to read and offer in evidence an endless parade of messages. The district attorney listened as patiently as he could for the first few hours. Finally, exasperated, he fairly shouted, "Enough of this. You will have all the time you'll need to present memos at the trial."

Hearing this, I shot off a motion calling for a halt to the grand jury investigation of my client. Obviously, I pointed out, the district attorney had already decided that my client should be indicted, since he assumed that my client would go to trial.

Result: My client was excused from that grand jury hearing.

It took two more grand-jury hearings before my client with his mountain of backup paper convinced the district attorney that life would be simpler without him on the premises.

It's not often that a client offers me the opportunity to do battle with government agencies and entrenched bureaucracies while protecting his rights as a scientist.

In this case of Dr. Robert Liefmann, his alleged crime was his successful treatment for crippling arthritis.

So how did a criminal lawyer like me—used to defending clients charged with serious crimes—get into this act? Here's how:

One day in 1968, Dr. Liefmann, a Canadian physician, asked me to work with his Canadian lawyers to solve a problem he was having with the Canadian Food and Drug Administration. Never one to avoid tangling with bureaucrats, domestic or foreign, I listened with interest.

Dr. Liefmann explained that he was treating patients suffering from arthritis and was having remarkable results. He used a combination of three drugs, all well known and approved by the FDA—prednisone, a powerful anti-inflammatory hormone; testosterone, the male tissue-building hormone; and estradiol, the tissue-building female hormone. Dr. Liefmann personally combined these three drugs to fit the specific needs of each patient.

The doctor based his treatment on his conclusion, arrived at after many years of research, that rheumatoid arthritis results from a hormone imbalance. A medication combining the correct proportion of hormones would, he proved, restore the balance and thus relieve the condition.

Before using his "hormone balance" techniques in his Canadian practice, Dr. Liefmann had done extensive research in Sweden and Mexico, and in Montreal hospitals. He had also successfully treated patients in Sweden with his methods.

His trouble with the Canadian FDA began when agents, posing as arthritics in pain, asked his secretary to send medicine to tide them over until an appointment could be made for an examination. The secretary sent the medicine as requested.

This, it turned out, was an unfortunate mistake. As a physician, Dr. Liefmann had a clear right to combine approved drugs—but only for use by his patients. Selling the combined drugs to others was a violation of Canada's Food and Drug Act—for which he was being prosecuted.

At the trial, we were able to show that all the hormones used were FDA-approved. Many of Dr. Liefmann's patients testified that the treatment had helped them greatly, allowing them to lead reasonably normal lives.

Eventually, the matter was settled satisfactorily. Dr. Liefmann agreed that he would supply the medication to his patients and to no one else and he returned, gratefully, to his work with arthritis victims.

But the battle with government bureaucracy over the hormone treatment wasn't over. Next, the United States government got involved. This chapter concerns an American physician, Dr. Elizabeth R. Daley.

While practicing family medicine in Bronxville, New York, Dr. Daley was struck by rheumatoid arthritis which gradually became so severe that she could barely lift a coffee cup. She consulted many specialists but they provided scant relief.

One day, her daughter read a story in *Look* magazine describing Dr. Liefmann's method of treatment. Hoping against hope, Dr. Daley traveled to Canada in 1962 to see Dr. Liefmann. To her intense joy and surprise, the treatments soon worked. Her pain subsided and she was able to resume her practice.

Eventually, she became Dr. Liefmann's associate in his research work and treatment of patients. In 1972, when he died, she carried on his work and helped open an Arthritis Medical Office in New York at the offices of the Institute for Research of Rheumatic Diseases.

Enter the United States Food and Drug Administration. On February 10, 1975, an FDA inspector appeared at Dr. Daley's offices in New York. The doctor was away, so the inspector questioned Donna Pinorsky, an R.N. employed there. He also served her with a Notice of Inspection. Nurse Pinorsky refused to answer any questions about the treatment administered and also refused to allow him to search the offices.

When told of this development, I called the inspector and asked what was going on. The FDA, he told me, was investigating Dr. Daley's alleged use of an unapproved drug, Liefcort.

A brief explanation is in order. Dr. Liefmann's medication, consisting of the three hormones already described, came to be loosely known as "Liefcort" only for a brief period of time. This name was immediately discontinued when Dr. Liefmann was told by the authorities that to market the product under this name required government approval. And of course in their investigation, the FDA had not found it listed among approved drugs. How could they? The name didn't exist.

We offered to resolve the matter in an open discussion. We offered to make full disclosure of the treatments and drugs used. Instead, the FDA made a second attempt to search Dr. Daley's offices. Again, Dr. Daley was away from the office and her nurse refused to allow it.

In the end, we were forced to go into a federal court to keep the FDA investigators away. This was a heavy experience for me. Here I was arrayed once more against my government, but this time in the unusual role of lawyer for the plaintiff.

This, you'd imagine, should have ended the affair. But, medical establishment and the government weren't through hounding us yet. The scene moved to Florida and the defendants included the Arthritis Foundation (Florida Chapter), the

Escambia County Medical Society and the Attorney General of Florida. Here's what happened:

On October 21, 1977, the Florida Attorney General, et al, sought an injunction to prevent the physician in charge of the Florida office using Dr. Liefmann's balanced hormone treatment—from

> doing or performing any act or course of conduct
> constituting the sale, offering to sell, delivery or
> offering to deliver the drug Liefcort to any person, or
> administering the said drug to any person or treating any
> person with the said drug, or offering to administer the said
> drug to any person or offering to treat any person with the
> said drug.

Statements by the defendants accompanying the application for injunction claimed the physician, attorney Henry Rothblatt, and others were about to "solicit customers to buy a dangerous drug," that the arthritis treatment administered by the physician constituted "an immediate and severe hazard and danger to the health" of patients, that the components of the medication administered by the physician were "new drugs" not approved by the FDA, and that they were "highly dangerous."

In response, we were able to show that over 30,000 patients had safely received treatment during the past twenty-five years, that all of the component medications used were FDA approved, and that none was a "new drug."

We also pointed out that the defendants failed to search major medical journals or to consult medical experts to discover whether the ingredients of the hormonal balance treatment were in fact FDA-approved. Defendants also failed to know that the physician had a legal right to combine approved drugs in treating his patients.

At long last, in May 1978, United States District Judge Norman C. Roettger ruled that "plaintiffs have sufficiently alleged the deprivation of federal constitutional rights under color of state law to state a claim."

Soon afterwards, the Arthritis Foundation, along with all

the government agencies and medical societies involved, agreed before a federal judge that the Arthritis Medical Center and its physicians and staff had a perfectly legal right to administer its treatment to patients in the successful way they had for years.

The government agencies and their lackeys further agreed before the federal judge that they would not interfere with the center's treatment of its patients. Otherwise, they would be faced with a multimillion dollar damage suit.

EIGHTEEN

What Happened to Justice?

THERE IS a case that continues to haunt me. I am convinced that the wrong man was convicted and is now serving a life sentence.

It involved a man I will call Frank Jones; using his real name might revive nightmarish memories for a number of people.

Maybe somewhere, sometime, the man I believe committed the crime for which Jones was convicted will read these words. If so, I fervently hope that he will be moved to come forward and tell the truth. It has happened before; perhaps it will again. If he should speak out, I promise that I will do everything in my power to get him every possible consideration in the courts.

I was not involved in the trial, though I wish I had been. I was retained to handle the appeal after a jury convicted Jones of murder in the first degree.

Back in the mid-1960s, Jones—a thirty-seven-year-old carpenter—had a lot going for him but even more going against him. In his favor, he was a hard-working family man with a wife and two daughters. Against him, a "confession" he gave to three of Long Island's most experienced detectives, describing one of the most brutal, sadistic sex murders in the history of Nassau County—the slaughter of a housewife. If she had not been stabbed to death, this poor woman would probably have died of fright: As she was being dragged upstairs to the bedroom, she soiled herself.

As I studied the record of the trial, I got my first inkling that something was very wrong—that it was a malign fate rather than guilt that put Jones behind bars.

Before sentencing him, the judge asked whether Jones had anything to say. This was his reply:

"I'm innocent and I never committed a crime in all my life. I always been a law-abiding citizen. The guilty party who committed this crime is running loose on the outside. This terrible mistake made by the police has taken the life of my mother. I was not even allowed to see her in the casket. You are sentencing an innocent man and his entire family."

An act? Perhaps, but I doubt it very much.

At the time, the police had been writhing under fierce criticism because of a large number of unsolved violent crimes on Long Island. They were flailing about wildly, hoping that blind luck would lead them to the killers. Once they came up with a suspect, public hysteria would do the rest. The murder for which Jones was convicted was so revolting in its details that no jury trying it could remain wholly objective. In such circumstances, the "presumption of innocence" often becomes a mockery.

It's my conviction that Jones happened to be in the wrong place at the wrong time. He had been picked up on suspicion of molesting a child, and he was at Rikers Island jail awaiting disposition of the case. What better murder suspect could the police hope for than an alleged child molester? Without warning, detectives dropped in on him and questioned him, together and in relays, for eight hours, pitting their sharp investigative skills against his own much slower mental processes. Adding to his plight, Jones was a diabetic. Deprived of his medication, with no one to counsel him, he would soon be ready to agree to almost anything.

Earlier, I described the time-honored techniques used to build a confession in the Mayronne case. I feel that suggestion, deceit, and intimidation were employed in this case as well.

The damnable thing about these confessions is that they sound so genuine. Specific details abound. How could a jury suspect that Jones's confession, so rich in incriminating detail, was not given of his own free will, without coercion, coaching or drilling? And the detective, after all, looked so clean and honest, so much the picture of outraged law and order.

Sometimes, the police go a bit too far. The confession ends up sounding too pat, too well edited. A guilty defendant tends to forget things, repeat himself, ramble. There are minor inconsistencies in his story, just as there are in life. The manufactured confession tries to rebut every claim of innocence and to reinforce every charge of guilt. It hopes to tie up the indisputable proof of guilt in one neat, tidy package. While you read Jones's confession as presented in court, judge for yourself whether or not the story has the ring of truth.

DETECTIVE: I asked him if he had anything else to tell us about any incident that he might have done in Nassau County. And at that time he said that he knew that he needed help. And I told him that I didn't know how to help him unless he told me what was bothering him. And then it was at this time that he said that he did something bad in Long Island.

He was asked where in Long Island did he do this. And he said, in Great Neck.

He was asked how do you know it's Great Neck?

And he said, "I did work in Great Neck."

And then we asked him to tell us about the incident. And he told us that this one day, the exact day he couldn't remember, he left his home in Ozone Park.

We asked him what kind of car he had and he said he had a 1961 Ford suburban wagon, color gray. And he left his home in Ozone Park in this station wagon and he was driving out to Long Island to a job. Somewhere while enroute to Long Island he saw some woman fixing her stocking on the street and this got him excited. So he continued on to work and he got on the Long Island Expressway heading east towards Long Island. And I believe it was on Lakeville Road he made a turn.

He got off the Expressway and he drove down to Northern Boulevard and Lakeville Road where he stopped for a traffic signal light. He then made a right turn on Northern Boulevard and he continued east for a short distance, and then he made another turn left somewhere into a residential area and he drove around for a while.

He didn't remember how long it was until he came to a residential area that had better than average homes. And as he was driving through this area, he came to a street where he observed a woman by some garbage cans. This woman he stated was dressed in, scantily dressed in a bathrobe and a nightgown.

He parked his car. He sat in the car and he watched this woman and he became excited and he started to play with himself. He watched this woman and the woman then went into a house.

He stated that he continued sitting in his station wagon. He continued to play with himself. And then he got out of this station wagon and he proceeded to walk towards this house that he saw the woman go into . . . Then he said that he went up to the front door of this house, rang the bell, he waited, and a woman that he saw out at the garbage cans came and opened the door. He then pushed the door and put his foot in and forced his way in. And the woman asked him what he wanted. And he said to her that "I want to make love to you." And with that he forced his way into the foyer.

And he stated that the woman started to holler and scream. And it was at this time that he hit her. And she fell to the foyer floor. He didn't know whether she was unconscious or not at this time.

He then stated that he went into the kitchen and he was asked where was this kitchen located. And he said to his right.

And he then stated that he went through some kitchen drawers and he found a knife. He was asked what kind of knife was it. And he said that he believed it was a paring knife.

He was asked what color was the knife. And he believed, he stated he believed it had a black handle. He took this knife and he went back to the foyer where this woman was laying and he forced her up some stairs into a bedroom. And she started to resist him and holler.

And it was then that he stated that he believed he hit her with something. We asked him what he hit her with and he thought it was something made of glass. . . . After he remembered hitting her with something made of glass, she fell to the floor and it was then that he kneeled down on the floor and he lifted her nightgown and bathrobe exposing her privates, and he then unzipped his pants, took out his penis, and he laid on top of her.

I asked him, he was asked how long did he lay on top of her. He said for about five minutes. He didn't recall whether he reached a climax or not. . . . While he was laying on top of her he started hitting her. He had the knife in his hands and he started hitting her about the shoulder. And at that time he thought that he had the knife in his hand with the handle, holding the handle, but when he saw blood he got excited and he got off and he cleaned himself off.

And then he took off his gloves. He believes he left them in the bedroom. And he didn't recall what he did with the knife but he believed he left the knife there also. And then after he cleaned himself off, he went to a dresser drawer which was in the bedroom and began looking for panties, ladies' panties. He didn't recall whether he found any. Then he saw a jewelry box on the dresser and he stated that he took some—an engagement ring, a sort of a charm bracelet, and some other jewelry which he put in his pocket.

We asked him why he took this, and he said he didn't know. He never did anything like that before. And he then went down into the kitchen where he saw some ladies' pocketbooks on top of the counters.

He stated that he went through these bags and he found a wallet which he also put in his pocket. And I believe he stated he took about $10 or $15 out of his pocket, out of this wallet.

He then left the house. He stated he was in the house for about 25 or 30 minutes and then he left the house the same way that he came in which was through the front door.

On his way home, he went up Hook Creek Boulevard where he stopped his car in the area that had large—it was a large area of garbage dumps. He then got out of his car and took this jewelry which he said was—he put in the bag under the front seat and he threw it into this large dumping area along Rockaway Boulevard.

He then got back in this station wagon and drove home.

He went up to Rockaway Boulevard and when he came to Conduit Avenue, he made a turn and he noticed that he had other pieces of jewelry still laying on the floor of his station wagon.

He said he picked up these pieces of jewelry and he came to a sewer or a catchbasin where he threw them in. That was the remaining pieces that he found on the floor of the car. He then drove home and when he got out of his car he took the clothes that he was wearing and he put them in a garbage can because he stated that the next day he knew the garbage would be picked up.

This is only part of the detectives' story. On the strength of this story alone the jury found Jones guilty. There was *no* other evidence against him.

There was much in the confession that did not ring true. A criminal lawyer develops a sixth sense about these things after a while. To get at the truth, I asked the court to give Jones a lie detector test. I also asked that Jones be given Amytal, a so-called truth drug. The district attorney objected, and the court turned me down.

Meanwhile, I kept finding more and more contradictions between the confession and the known facts. These are a few:

- The confession stated that after committing the murder, Jones went to 258 Jerome Avenue in Mineola to do some carpentry work. At the trial it was established that he did not go there at all.
- The confession stated that Jones had discarded jewelry taken from the house, in a dump in Queens and in a storm sewer drain. At the trial it was established that no jewelry was found at either location.
- The confession stated that the murder knife had a black handle. At the trial it was established that it had a silver handle.
- The confession stated that Jones had taped the victim's hands. At the trial it was established that her hands were not taped when the body was found.
- The confession stated that he stabbed the victim four or five

times. At the trial it was established that she had been stabbed some seventy times or more.

- The confession stated that the house was of a colonial type. It was established that the house was a split level. As a carpenter, Jones would have known the difference.
- The confession stated that Jones parked his car in the street near the victim's house. At the trial, in spite of a massive investigation, no witness was presented who saw his car near the house.
- The confession stated that after the crime Jones went to a lumber yard to change into work pants. At the trial the proprietor of the lumber yard could not recall seeing Jones in the yard that day. Neither could an employee.
- A sketch of the murder scene allegedly drawn by Jones showed garbage cans in front of the house. And the confession stated that Jones decided to commit the crime when he was driving by the victim's house and saw her, scantily clad, at the garbage cans at front. At the trial it was established that there were no garbage cans in front of the house.
- The sketch showed the woman's feet toward the bedroom door. At the trial it was established that her head was protruding from the doorway.

All of this confusion could not have been caused by Jones. In my mind, it was the inevitable result of mixups among the detectives, each one determined to outdo the others in building an airtight case.

The business of the garbage cans is fascinating. The police even got Jones to draw a diagram of the scene, garbage cans and all. The police are very big on diagrams. They look so scientific and convincing. But this was a luxury home in a classy area. The residents would not dream of leaving garbage cans lining the streets as in New York City. Cans are left in garages or back yards. The detectives of course did not live in luxury homes. Very few policemen did, except for a few members of the New York Narcotics Squad. So it was quite natural for them to assume that garbage cans would be lined up at the street. Garbage cans therefore became part of the confession and were included in the diagram Jones drew, under expert guidance.

Jones was such a mild man, eager to please, worried about his delayed insulin shot. It's easy to picture him saying everything the detectives were eager to have him say, and more. Those cops probably never had a more obliging suspect.

After some study, the statement the detectives claim Jones gave them becomes surrealistic. You sense that Jones has been answering "yes" to questions like "Is this what happened?", "Is that what happened next?" Then the "yes" is expanded by the police into a full, formal statement repeating all the details supplied in the questions.

For example, let's assume the detective asks Jones, off the record, "Did you see a couple of purses?" To oblige, Jones answers, "Yes." This exchange eventually appears in the record this way. "Jones said, 'I think I saw a couple of purses down there.'"

To the jury it seems clear that it was Jones who brought up the matter of the purses.

And so it goes, on and on for eight hours, until the whole thing is neatly wrapped up. If New York had had the death penalty, Jones would surely have gone to the chair.

There were several defense witnesses who cast real doubt on the prosecution's case. There was testimony that Jones was actually somewhere else when the crime was committed. There was testimony that he was strangely spotless after he was supposed to have murdered the victim. This, when the prosecution pictured him as wallowing in blood. His car too showed no evidence of blood.

But none of this did any good. At a certain point in a trial, there is nothing anyone can do or say that will dispel the atmosphere of guilt that has been created.

To a lawyer who has read a lot of court records, there was another strange fact about the Jones case. During an important interrogation, there is usually a correction officer, prison guard, or other non-police official present. This witness to the questioning generally testifies at the trial on the defendant's demeanor, on how the questions were put, how the defendant answered, how he looked, and so on. There was no attempt at the trial to present anyone who witnessed any part of the questioning. Nothing, nothing but the self-serving statements of the detectives.

But there is no point in going on with this. When all is said and done, it is the jury that has the last word on the facts. Appeals courts will not set aside the jury's verdict unless there is proof of clear error or abuse. So Jones is still in prison, hoping against hope that the man who killed the Long Island housewife may yet come forward. I join him in that hope.

NINETEEN

Counselor–Take the Stand

W HEN I started writing this book, there were so many things I wanted to say about criminal law, points I felt impelled to make, suggestions to young lawyers and would-be lawyers. Now that I am reaching the end, it occurs to me that I have covered a good deal, but that there's a lot more that hasn't found its way into the manuscript.

To remedy this, here are some of the questions I am most frequently asked by clients, students in my classes, and other lawyers at symposia, meetings, and similar forums, along with answers that I will try to make clear and satisfactory.

The public tends to see plea bargaining as a way to cheat justice. What can be done?

The "reformers" who issue public statements about the evils of plea bargaining need to do a little simple arithmetic. If every case went to trial, the courts—already struggling to keep up with their flood of cases—would stagger under the unmanageable load. We would need more judges, more prosecutors, more lawyers, more courthouses, at enormous cost to taxpayers.

But more to the point—the fact is that plea bargaining generally produces substantial justice. After all, a prosecutor who has an open-and-shut case is not going to offer a plea. And a defense lawyer who feels his case is strong and the prosecutor's full of holes is not going to accept one.

During the give-and-take between prosecution and defense an accommodation is reached acceptable to both, and to the judge as well.

This process of negotiation, a time-honored one, offers

199

advantages to both sides. The defendant pleads guilty to a lesser charge and receives a lighter sentence than he might after a trial; the prosecutor adds a conviction to his record. And the trial is washed off the court's crowded calendar, cleanly and in most cases, fairly.

Do you find newspaper, TV, and radio reporters accurate and helpful?

When a lawyer is involved in a spectacular case, he quickly discovers that amazing clan, the reporters. Lesson number one: A reporter thinks nothing of waking you at 3 A.M. with a question he feels is vital. He sounds surprised to find you asleep.

I am probably the reporters' biggest fan among criminal lawyers. That is why I never say "No comment," that safe but silly answer to a reporter's question. If I can't hand out any hard information, I try at least to supply something usable.

Mind you, I'm not being philanthropic. I have found that I often learn more from the reporters than they do from me. I sense when their questions are based on information they have obtained from the prosecutor's office or from some concerned politician. This can be very helpful. I try to reciprocate by letting the reporters know when they are veering off the track, usually because of misinformation they were fed by someone on the other side.

One of the reasons White House spokesmen have had such a hard time in recent years is that the reporters no longer trust them. For the most part, the spokesmen are the scapegoats for their bosses' deceitful practices, and they shoulder the brunt of the reporters' resentment.

I find it a lot harder to match wits with reporters than with judges or other lawyers. The men and women of the media have been around. They have met and observed every kind of human being and they are not taken in by charm or rhetoric. When I notice that media people have acquired a distaste for someone, I am immediately on my guard against that person. There's sure to be something wrong with him.

By and large, I regard reporters as Hamlet did actors: "Let them be well used, for they are the abstract and brief chronicles of the time. After your death you were better have a bad epitaph than their ill report while you live."

At a time when government has tremendous resources and doesn't skimp in their use—1,500 FBI men and various other kinds of gumshoes were assigned to the Watergate break-in and subsequent events—you need the help the media can give you. Sometimes they know more than you do about your own client. For example, it was Les Whitten, Jack Anderson's brilliant and personable associate, who helped spill the beans on ITT and other national horrors.

There was a time, though, I admit, when I took a dim view of the accuracy of what I read in the papers. Whenever I had firsthand knowledge of the subject covered, I seemed to find errors of fact as well as of interpretation in the stories.

Back in the twenties and thirties, there were often deliberate falsifications, as well. A veteran reporter I know stated that there were a couple of reporters in Brooklyn whose specialty was creating fictitious news stories. Whenever there was a dearth of genuine news, they would fill the void with holdups, fires, human-interest pieces, none of which had happened, except in their heads. Some people, my friend added, thought it a bit strange that they hadn't known of the holdup right in their neighborhood. But, human nature being what it is, others were always ready to say, "Sure, I was right there. I saw the whole thing."

Nowadays, I notice, reporters really bear down in important cases and come up with amazingly accurate accounts of complicated matters, and with perceptive insights as well. Probably, the challenge of difficult situations brings out the best in them. Maybe some have visions of a Pulitzer Prize to spur them on.

While I was still wrestling with the aftermath of Watergate, *The New York Times* devoted an entire issue of its Sunday Magazine Section to a summary of the case by J. Anthony Lukas, who already had the Prize to his credit. Lukas saved me about $25,000 in time and a great deal of mental effort by his masterly roundup of the facts, evidence, issues and personalities involved in the case.

I hasten to add that this is not a legally collectible debt.

How dependable are criminal identifications?

Recall, if you will, the times you thought you saw a friend on the street and then realized when you got closer that you were mistaken. Not surprising when you realize that it's inevitable that some people will resemble each other. Among friends, this can be embarrassing or amusing. But when it leads to the conviction of an innocent person in court, it's tragic.

At a seminar I moderated, Judge Nathan Sobel of the Brooklyn Supreme Court said: "I am convinced that in our state prisons there is a good percentage of persons who are absolutely innocent. They are there because of a faulty identification."

I strongly agree. From time to time, the papers carry stories about a man identified by witness after witness as guilty of a crime. Eventually, by pure chance, the real culprit is caught and the innocent man cleared.

The surprising thing is that, even after they are shown actual proof of the man's innocence, some of the witnesses stick to their identifications. Why? Probably for the same reason they made the identification in the first place: a resemblance, desire to be the center of attention or sympathy, the inability to admit a mistake.

Judge Sobel believes that identification is the weakest, not—as commonly supposed—the strongest part of a case. There is much too great a chance of error in any identification based on facial or physical characteristics. This danger, added to the occasional adroit brainwashing by the police, has caused many a miscarriage of justice. A jury that convicts a man on the basis of identification alone is playing Russian Roulette with a man's liberty, sometimes with his life.

In a related area, experiments have shown that a person's recollection of an observed event is about 60 percent accurate after twenty-four hours. A week later, accuracy has dropped to 50 percent; a month later, 40 percent; six months later, 25 percent. After three years, the degree of accuracy is virtually zero.

Witnesses at the various My Lai trials and hearings were, I am convinced, largely under the power of suggestion. Noncoms were told what their superiors had testified and pretty soon they were repeating the same stories. One of the purposes of cross-examination is to find out how much of a witness's story comes out of his own knowledge and how much is a repetition of what he heard from others.

Former Vice President Agnew brought the term nolo contendere *into the language. What does it mean?*

Literally it means "I do not wish to contest." The *nolo contendere* plea admits for the specific case the charges made against the defendant. Some jurisdictions permit this plea. Others, including New York, do not. But the federal courts do.

In New York, a kind of guilty plea is allowed which is the equivalent of *nolo contendere.* For want of a better name, it is called an "Alford Plea."

The name stems from *Alford* vs. *United States* in which Chief Justice Warren Burger said that pleas of guilty may be entered by defendants as part of the plea-bargaining process, but that this does not mean defendants must admit guilt.

The rationale is this. Suppose the defendant has been charged with murder. He possibly could face the electric chair. The D.A. offers a plea of guilty calling for a life sentence instead of the chair. The defendant says, in effect, "Look, I didn't do it, but I'm afraid I'll be convicted wrongly and sent to the electric chair. So I'll plead guilty but I won't say I did it because I did not."

Such a plea is possible, but only to expedite the plea-bargaining negotiations. It's as though A sues B. B knows he doesn't owe A a dime. But B's lawyer says, "You don't know what the judge or jury may do, so let's give A a couple of bucks." And B says, "All right, I don't like it but I'll settle. But I won't admit I owe him anything."

Here is how it works in court. As the defendant's lawyer, I

say to the judge, "Your honor, under *Alford* vs. *United States*, the defendant wishes to plead guilty to _____ charge. I want the record to reflect that by entering this plea of guilty, we do not admit any of the underlying facts as set forth in the indictment. We are merely entering this plea of guilty in the interests of justice to bring about a disposition of this case." Period.

So you see, the net result is the same as in *nolo contendere*.

Why are legal fees so high?

This is a fairly touchy subject, what with the Internal Revenue Service on the lookout for clues leading to people they think are making gobs of money. Accordingly, I was less than thrilled when *Time*, terming me a "lawyer's lawyer" and a "voluble, flamboyant and highly skilled criminal specialist," said that I had charged my Watergate defendants $125,000.

I admit to voluble, even flamboyant, but not to getting the money. As every lawyer knows, "chargin' ain't getting'." Lest IRS get any big ideas, I collected only about $18,000 and that didn't even cover my expenses.

Unhappily, the lawyer doesn't get to pocket that big fee he charges, even if he collects it. There are enormous costs and time-consuming tasks involved in researching and preparing the best possible defense. You have to hire investigators, have transcripts made, question all witnesses, prepare endless motions, briefs, and other documents. I won't bore you with the sad story of inflated rents, electricity and phone bills.

I profess to believe that the laborer is worthy of his hire, though I don't go as far as my delightful friend, the great Texas criminal lawyer, Percy Foreman. When asked how he could justify getting confessed murderers off, Percy said, in his rolling tones, "Mah fees are their punishment."

When I am able to battle the odds and keep a man from spending most of his remaining years in prison, I feel that I should be paid adequately. Especially when the man goes back to making a handsome living, sometimes legitimately.

Like most criminal lawyers, I have had the exasperating experience of gaining a hard-won acquittal only to have the defendant use the promised fee for a trip to the Bahamas with a couple of girlfriends.

One last note. Lawyers have a way of getting emotionally involved in their cases. Not infrequently, they sink their own money into paying for appeals and other expenses, partly for their client's sake but mostly to vindicate their own judgment.

Are lineups fair? Who are the people chosen?

Elizabeth Loftis discussed this problem in a number of lectures. She included a photo of an actual lineup out West that showed four whites and one black. The sheriff claimed that "These are typical people in our town."

Sometimes the authorities try to be fair and bring out prisoners for a lineup. In one case I defended, the victim identified one of the prisoners in the lineup as the perpetrator.

Almost anyone who happens to be around can be used in a lineup. Sometimes they are cops or clerks. Practically anyone will do.

Do you favor the death penalty?

I consider myself very lucky that during the years that we had capital punishment in New York, no client of mine went to the chair. There has been widespread sentiment recently for the return of the death penalty, outlawed partially by the United States Supreme Court as "cruel and unusual punishment," and in violation of the Constitution. We had plenty of serious crime when we had the death penalty. I see no reason to believe that crime has decreased in the states where it has been restored.

Lawyers have described to me the nightmarish scenes in the town of Ossining during the hours before the execution at Sing Sing prison, now known as the Ossining Correctional Facility.

The condemned man's loved ones—almost everyone has someone to whom he is still the lovable child of yesterday—would go to the prison for a last heartrending farewell. They would spend the last seconds hoping against hope for a miraculous reprieve. Many relatives and friends would drink themselves into a state of wild hilarity which exploded into hysteria at the fatal hour.

A good number of the convicted murderers protested their innocence to the last. This troubled those who did not understand what the convicts meant by "innocent." Most of the condemned never quite appreciated, no matter how often it was explained to them, that if they had taken part in a holdup in which a man was killed, they were just as guilty in the eyes of the law as the man who pulled the trigger.

There were cases in which as many as four men were executed for a single crime. The three who had not fired died convinced that a terrible mistake was being made.

The New York State Penal Law makes this felony-murder-participation rule a little less harsh. A defendant who can show that he did not actively take part in a murder can sometimes avoid conviction for the murder—although not, of course, for the underlying felony.

Some condemned criminals had truly bizarre ideas about the law. One lawyer told me of a client who died swearing that he was innocent because the holdup victim lunged at him in spite of the loaded gun he held. "What could I do?" the defendant asked. "It was his own fault."

During the Depression of the thirties, there was much bitterness against society among the more articulate convicts. "When I needed a few dollars," one man told his lawyer, "there was no one around. Now when I'm dying, all the do-gooders are here." This unfortunate had joined in a holdup to get money for a suit of clothes so that he could apply for a job. He stole $35, got the job, and was arrested and later convicted. A job, not murder, was on his mind. But he paid dearly for his mistake.

Have you ever represented a client in an entrapment case? What is entrapment, anyway?

The Abscam trials have dramatized the issue of entrapment, but misconceptions still survive.

The general rule is that the government may use informers

to trap a wrongdoer—*only* if the government has information about the suspect's prior inclination to the crime involved. In other words, the government may *not* set a trap to catch someone who never showed any inclination towards the crime suspected.

I now represent Mel Weinberg, self-acclaimed Super Con Man, who informed for the FBI in the Abscam affair. In addition, I have represented a number of clients who did double duty by informing for the government.

Most people are unaware of the large role played by informers in law enforcement. As in the Abscam trials, the government is often aware—or at least strongly suspects—that certain individuals are carrying on illegally. But how to get enough solid evidence that will stand up in court?

Often, the answer is informers—people in the suspect's own business, or agents sufficiently skilled and knowledgeable to pass. These informers set up the suspect so that the FBI, Narcotics Bureau, Customs Office, or whatever agency is involved can catch their quarry in the midst of a criminal act.

The result, while salutary to society, is often less so to the informer. He has stuck his neck way out and survived in a world where informers often end up, tied in gunny sacks, at the bottom of the sea. Their idea of a proper reward for all this is usually more generous than what the government had in mind. The government, meanwhile, feels that the informer has not done nearly enough.

For example, a client I'll call Frank Johnson arranged a perfectly legal insurance plan for members of a union. All went well until one day a delegation from the union appeared. Where was their "envelope," they wanted to know. What could Johnson do? He paid off and gave them their kickback.

Predictably, Johnson was soon picked up and indicted for conspiracy to milk the insurance company through bribery payments.

At this point, the FBI stepped in. How would Johnson like to help them get evidence on the union officials? In return, the government would be eternally grateful and would take a sympathetic look at that bribery indictment facing Johnson.

Johnson said O.K., and at great risk to life and limb helped send a few crooked union officials away.

But then the aftermath. Johnson felt that the government let him down. The least he expected was that the Feds would restore him to the luxury of his former financial state. But no, that wouldn't do, said the Feds. If he looked prosperous, his credibility in future trials against the union officials would be lost. Everyone would assume that he had been paid off for his testimony!

Can you give an example of false evidence?

Lloyd Eldon Miller, Jr. was convicted of raping and killing an eight-year-old girl. He spent seven years in the Illinois death house. *Time* called it "a classic case of false evidence."

The prosecutor passed off on the jury a pair of Miller's shorts as bloodstained, knowing all the time that the "blood" was really paint. One prospective witness, Miller's landlady, knew that Miller had been asleep in his room when the crime was committed. She was told that she had a constitutional right not to testify. The prosecutor was much less concerned about Miller's constitutional rights, keeping him locked up for fifty-two hours without access to friend, relative, or lawyer.

After this beginning, the prosecutor and the police went on to bully and confuse witnesses. They told Miller that a pubic hair found in the girl's vagina had been proved to be his. It was actually someone else's. They wrote out a detailed confession for him to sign and performed other little services which landed Miller within spitting distance of the electric chair.

The unfortunate defendant was so beaten down by this concentration of official malice and fraud that twice he had to be moved from death row to the psychiatric ward. It was only by the grace of God and the devotion of his parents that Miller finally got a stay for a habeas corpus hearing. The stay came just seven days before the time set for the electrocution. The whole story is told in a United States Supreme Court opinion.

The Miller case was extreme, but there have been plenty of others almost as bad. Unfortunately, the defendants are frequently too poor, too ignorant, or too frightened to do anything about it.

If they cry their outrage in prison, they are met with, "Sure, sure, you're innocent—so is everyone else here." In the more civilized prisons, they no longer get a knock on the head to bring them to a more sensible outlook. But even that is not lacking in some jurisdictions.

Discussing the Miller case, *Time* wondered why prosecutors were not themselves jailed for such frameups. A good question. Unfortunately, they never are. I suppose it is silly to expect a district attorney to establish a precedent that might boomerang against him some day.

Is the lie detector a useful device for criminal lawyers?

Perhaps because of my friendship with F. Lee Bailey, the lie detector's greatest champion, I have a lot of faith in the polygraph, which is the scientific term for the device. Though many courts still do not admit evidence of polygraph findings, I find it very useful in interviewing clients.

If your client doesn't tell you the whole truth, you are behind the eight ball. When I sense that a client may be holding back, I say to him that it would be a good idea for him to take a polygraph test "just for the record."

"Are these things really accurate?" he asks.

"Yes."

He digests this and begins to tell the true story.

A lot of people have the idea that if they tell their lawyer all the bad things they did, he will be less likely to help them. They imagine that a lawyer represents only innocent people, so they try to act innocent.

It's easy to understand the reticence of some defendants to talk freely even to their lawyer. If I interview a young man in the presence of his parents, he will usually be very reluctant to open up. So I get the young fellow alone where he can "spill his guts" out of earshot of his parents.

When I was representing Colonel Oran Henderson, the commander of the brigade made notorious by Lieutenant William Calley, against charges that he had covered up the My

Lai Massacre, I had him take three polygraph tests administered by acknowledged experts. I was not surprised that he
passed with flying colors every time.

Is being intoxicated a viable defense?

Where intent is a necessary element of a crime—as in
murder—the intoxication defense is raised as negating that
requirement. The judge will rule along these lines: "Ordinarily, intoxication is no defense, but if the defendant was so
drunk that he didn't know what he was doing . . . then intent
to kill was not there."

This defense will generally lower the degree of the crime in
proved homicide cases. A killing without the requisite
intent—committed while intoxicated—may be treated as
manslaughter rather than murder two.

Can news stories prejudice a defendant's case?

Mark Twain once said that the most horrible experience a
person could have was to be pilloried in print for the first time.
Gareth Martinis had good reason to agree with Twain when
his case was on the front pages almost daily, some years back.

You may recall that the Bronx youth, a son of a New York
State Supreme Court justice, drove his car into another vehi-
cle, causing the death of five persons.

To the public the case was cut and dried: The young man
was guilty of homicide and deserved a long prison term.

When the district attorney and the courts did not oblige, the
newspapers charged them with a long list of shortcomings and
worse, including incompetence and political chicanery. Because of the father's position, the public was able to give its
imagination full rein, visualizing backroom deals, political
strong-arming, and similar routine fantasies.

Ironically, while such occurrences are not uncommon, they
were definitely not necessary in the Martinis case. Let me tell
you why.

Every criminal lawyer realizes that it is easy to defend
against an automobile manslaughter charge. In fact, the word-
ing of the law in such cases makes it difficult for the defense to
lose. In order to convict, the prosecutor must prove the of-

fender guilty of "culpable negligence," a phrase which the New York courts have construed to mean the wild, reckless behavior of a man out to kill himself and everybody else without regard for the consequences.

To pin such a label on a driver immediately after a tragic accident is easy to do. But it is a different story in the quiet of a courtroom days or weeks afterwards. In fact, I can recall just three convictions for automobile homicide during all my years of practice. In the same interval, there were scores of acquittals and many more cases in which the driver was convicted of a lesser offense and fined or had his license suspended.

The district attorneys and the judges are well aware of the situation, of course, and have become more or less reconciled to it. The truth is that they treated the Martinis case as they would any other, and they were genuinely surprised and horrified when the storm broke.

Political figures, on or off the bench, are timid by nature. Everyone began immediately trying to justify himself when no justification was called for.

Later on, the three Criminal Court judges who were fiercely criticized for conferring only five minutes before acquitting Martinis, tried in vain to convey to the public the simple truth. In that court, with its crowded calendar of misdemeanors, judges do not ordinarily confer for anything like five minutes about any one case. They usually glance at each other out of the corner of an eye, take a quick consensus and render their decision right at the bench. But try to explain that to a public and press screaming for blood!

As I watched the judges absorb their daily dose of abuse, I felt that the fault lay, partly at least, in the fact that none of the reporters or editors knew anything about the law, and had no interest in learning. The papers would not dream of letting a scientific simpleton cover important medical or scientific news, but they had no problem with sending a legal illiterate to write about significant legal cases and proceedings. The best story from their point of view, the journalistic point of view, was the one that put the authorities in the worst possible light.

Some of the better newspapers have realized this weakness

and have tried to remedy the situation. *The New York Times,* for instance, encouraged Anthony Lewis to apply for a Nieman Fellowship to Harvard Law School so that he might learn what the law was all about. It paid off handsomely. Lewis became the ace Supreme Court reporter. His book, *Gideon's Trumpet,* describing the case in which the Court laid down the rule that every defendant is entitled to counsel, became a national best seller.

At the time of the Martinis case, I was chairman of The Criminal Courts Committee of the Bronx County Bar Association, and I pointed out in a letter to *The New York Times* that the decision of the three judges was correct. Public clamor notwithstanding, there was no legal evidence to sustain the charges.

Have you had a young client who was arrested for possession of narcotics?

As a reaction to some savage sentences imposed on young people, most courts have become more lenient in their treatment of kids found with small quantities of marijuana, hashish, and other drugs. Even so, judges cannot ignore the evidence in such cases and are pleased when a lawyer can give them a legal out.

Cases involving possession of drugs by youngsters are won usually if at all because of "unlawful search and seizure," arising out of "a lack of probable cause." Explanation: A cop cannot stop your car without good reason and order you to open the trunk for his inspection. If he does and finds drugs there, the evidence is inadmissable.

To beat this prohibition, some cops come up with far-out stories. One young client of mine was stopped by a policeman for no apparent reason other than his long hair. The cop ordered him to open the trunk, found some marijuana, and arrested the boy.

The policeman had obviously had some briefing on the subject of illegal search and seizure. In court, he told the judge that when he stopped the car, the boy said to him: "If you don't believe me, search the trunk."

The judge stared at the policeman for a minute and then threw out the case without further ado.

The situation has improved somewhat since ballplayers and construction workers have begun to let their hair grow. But there was a time not so long ago when long hair and a beard could get you in trouble in just about any part of the country.

After a while, the pushers and heavy users switched to the equivalent of crew cuts and enjoyed practical immunity for their operations. In the old days, a crook would grow a beard to disguise himself. Today, he takes off his beard for the same purpose.

Remember Arthur Bremmer, the man who crippled Governor Wallace? He was able to get right up close to his victim because he looked like the All-American Boy.

In the Russell case, you made good use of coram nobis. *What precisely is that?*

If you want to withdraw a guilty plea, you generally do so before sentencing. However, there are times when you want to withdraw the plea after sentence is imposed. This is where the famous writ of error *coram nobis* comes in.

For example, I represented a young Puerto Rican who was already serving a ten-to-twenty-year sentence when I took over his case. His mother came to me and told me that her son's lawyer had promised that the boy would get a light sentence if he pleaded guilty. Apparently, the defendant spoke no English and the lawyer spoke no Spanish. The defendant claimed that the only time he understood what the lawyer said to him was one occasion when the lawyer spoke through an interpreter. At that time, he said, "Don't worry. I'll get you Elmira Reformatory."

I argued in my motion for a writ of error *coram nobis* to set aside the conviction, that the transcript of the plea of guilty was incorrect, that the court's minutes did not truly reflect what the defendant said and what was said by the attorneys, the judge, and the various parties to the proceeding, including the interpreter. I maintained that the actual words spoken to the defendant were critical, as were his responses in Spanish, if we were to determine whether he knew he was pleading guilty and that he might get ten to twenty years in prison.

I added that all we had in the record was the translation of the questions put to the defendant. There was no way to determine whether the translations into Spanish were accurate; "the defense contends that what appears on the record is not in fact what was said."

The judge asked me how I thought such a situation could be prevented. I said that either the court reporters should keep a record of the precise words spoken, or a tape recording should be made.

The judge said that he didn't think the courts were prepared to handle it. My motion for a writ of error *coram nobis* was denied.

This old-fashioned court procedure still exists today. However, tape recordings are made in federal court when pleas of guilty are taken to provide a backup for the court reporter.

Do the police unwittingly violate the rights of suspects?

The greatest favor an arresting officer can do for a defendant is to violate his constitutional rights. If he doesn't allow him to call a lawyer, for example, the case may go down the drain then and there. Most cops are by now alert to the danger and bend over backwards to give the defendant all his rights. And the new breed of policeman is better educated and trained. However, there are still enough dumb or stubborn cops around to gladden the heart of defendants everywhere and give their lawyers an easy win in court.

Here's an example of how the thoughtlessness and ignorance of a policeman can turn a case around.

I represented a man and his wife in a serious narcotics case. A large quantity of heroin was found in their apartment.

After arresting the couple, the officer used the defendant's phone to call the *Daily News* in New York. He told the *News* that the defendants' child had carried the narcotics. The story duly appeared with the headline, CHILD ASSISTING PARENTS IN CARRYING NARCOTICS.

On the day of the trial, I made a motion to dismiss the

indictment on the grounds that the police had tainted the trial and poisoned the atmosphere with the publicity they generated at the time of the arrest.

The next day the D.A. made an offer. "I'll dismiss the charges against the wife and allow a plea to a misdemeanor for the man, with a little time to be served and probation or a suspended sentence."

Without the help of the stupid conduct of the police, the couple would probably have gone away for about ten years.

There is much concern over the administration of justice. What can be done?

To answer this fully would take another whole book. Let me set down a few of my general feelings on this vital subject.

First off, I don't believe that more police, more judges, more prisons, more lawyers are the complete answer. The trouble is deep and can't be solved by numbers alone. The whole system is inefficient in every aspect.

If you have a traffic system plagued by too many cars, ineffectual police, confusing traffic systems, then your traffic situation must be poor. This applies as well to a justice system.

To be efficient, our system must be revolutionized from the ground up. To begin with, the police waste a lot of time on pointless arrests. These bad arrests tie up a lot of time in court. A good police lieutenant should see to it that arrests without sufficient evidence are not made. And if they are made, they should be cleaned out before they clutter up the courts.

So you have all these unnecessary cases churning through the courts, handled in many instances by inefficient D.A.s, lawyers, and judges. Almost no one really tries very hard to make the system work better.

Court reform can be only as effective as the judges who run the courts. Fewer than one-third of the judges I have come before are really competent to do a good job. The other two-thirds know the law and understand the psychological and sociological problems involved in the cases they try. These judges grind out some semblance of justice.

After the sentencing, we reach another wasteland—prison.

The plight of those who cannot make the adjustment to prison life is far more than just pitiable. Maddened by confinement, they become dangerous to themselves and to others. When the prison administration is less than enlightened and prison guards regard themselves as zoo keepers, we have Atticas.

Without question, some prisoners are brutal and destructive. But prison reform is long overdue. Better pay for prison guards is an essential first step if we are to attract intelligent, qualified men to these jobs. Low pay makes the guard vulnerable to corruption. Poorly paid guards are also more likely to take out their resentment on the prisoners. Give the prison guard a better deal and he will give the prisoner one, too.

What do you consider the most dramatic moment in a trial?

The passing of the sentence is the moment of truth. This is so for lawyers as well as for defendants. If I ever quit the practice of law—God forbid—it will be because of the stress and strain of the sentence day, with the shaking defendant at my side and the terror-stricken family a few aisles back. Maybe it's because of the trauma of the sentencing that I fight tooth and nail to make it unnecessary.

In the old days, the lawyer would get up before the judge and launch into an impassioned plea for mercy. If the judge was in a merciful mood, the oratory worked. But it was of little value if the judge was (a) skeptical, (b) sleepy, or (c) mad at the lawyer.

Today, my procedure is to prepare a voluminous pre-sentencing plea to the judge in writing. Included are all the facts in the defendant's favor—his history, letters from former teachers, employers and clergymen; psychiatrists' statements, job offers, and other evidence of good character. I have found that this written plea goes far to counteract the court's own probation-department report, which is often heavily loaded against the defendant.

If I can make a convincing case that the defendant will be better off out of prison than in, and that society will not be imperiled by his being at large, most judges will go along.

Very few judges want to add a human being who might be

salvageable to the roster of inmates. Perhaps, when prisons offer rehabilitation instead of damnation, judges will not be so reluctant to send people there.

Do you ever think of going into politics?

In 1962, there was a story in the New York *Daily News,* describing me as a "real, live Perry Mason" or some such foolishness.

A friend called me and said, "Why don't you run as a reform candidate for Congress in the 21st District against James Healy [the incumbent Democrat]?"

My friend was organizing some reform clubs in the Bronx. He poi:ited out that the district was about 65 percent Jewish, 10 percent black, 15 percent Puerto Rican, and 10 percent Irish. He said, "You're a well-known lawyer in the Bronx. You speak Spanish. You could win in the Democratic primary as a reform candidate." So I went for it.

After I had been running for a while, along came Jim Scheuer, who told me that he was also going to run—and most important—that he had the necessary money for a real campaign.

A few days later, my friend called me again. "Henry, I don't think you can do battle with Scheuer with all his money," he said, adding, "Scheuer wants to put me on his payroll to work for him full time."

Soon afterwards, Scheuer's campaign manager and I had lunch. "You don't have a chance against all this money," he told me. "If you don't withdraw, both of you will lose and Healy will win."

I told him that they couldn't buy me off. Healy won. But Scheuer did win the next time.

So much for politics and me.

How do you view the government's attitude toward lawyers today?

These days you can win an awful lot of cases by keeping this one thing in mind: The government cannot willfully commit any act to damage the right of a defendant, or withhold evidence that can tend to exonerate him.

If the government should do this, the case must be dismissed.

Things will get tougher when the government breaks some of the bad habits it has developed in recent years. But from what I have been seeing lately, this reform is not imminent.

What if anything have you learned from the young people on your staff?

After our clients, the Lanes, were convicted, we appealed the case right up to the Supreme Court.

By the time we got to that tribunal, our legal arguments had been pretty well deflated by intermediate courts. We really didn't have much left to say.

One day, I was going through the file hoping for a new inspiration, when I came across this exchange of notes between my associate, Steve Peskin, and Ronald Schectman, a bright young law student then working in our office:

RON: See if we should have a brief reply. Check Sup. Ct. Rule #24. If you think so, throw something together and have it ready by next Friday. — Steve

STEVE: : Sup. Ct. Rule #24 makes a reply brief discretionary. Don't believe we have any more to say of merit, and it might be best not to try to bullshit the Supreme Court. — Ron

Often, when I'm undecided over arguments for a brief, I recall Ron's sage observation.